CLAIM YOUR FREE 30 SECOND PRESENTAT.

G000145087

Simply complete this coupon and send it to us to receive your fr presentation. Packed with tips and practical suggestions the 30 SECON MASTER helps you make first-class presentations every time.

☐ *I would like to receive further information on the Ready Made Activities Resource Packs*

Name: _____ Position: _____

Company/Organisation: _____

Address (including postcode): _____

_____

Country: _____

Telephone: _____ Fax: _____

Nature of business: _____

Title of book purchased: _____

Comments: _____

_____

------------------------------ | **Fold Here Then Staple** | ------------------------------

We would be very grateful if you could answer these questions to help us with market research.

1 Where/How did you hear of this book?
☐ in a bookshop
☐ in a magazine/newspaper
(please state which):

_____

☐ information through the post
☐ recommendation from a colleague
☐ other (please state which):

_____

2 Which newspaper(s)/magazine(s) do you read regularly?:

_____

_____

3 When buying a business book which factors influence you most?
(Please rank in order)
☐ recommendation from a colleague
☐ price
☐ content
☐ recommendation in a bookshop
☐ author
☐ publisher
☐ title
☐ other(s):

4 Is this book a
☐ personal purchase?
☐ company purchase?

**5 Would you be prepared to spend a few minutes talking to our customer services staff to help with product development?
YES/NO**

Claim your 30 Second Presentation Master
***FREE** from Pitman Publishing*

Simply complete the reverse of this coupon and send it to us – no stamp needed – to claim your FREE 30 SECOND PRESENTATION MASTER – packed with tips and practical suggestions to help make a first-class presentation every time.

Ready Made Activities Resource Packs

The really practical way to run YOUR coaching session. Each Resource Pack contains all the information you can find in the paperback Ready Made Activities... books, plus much, much more!

- **Free Video**
  Use it to introduce the session or reinforce your message
- **Overhead Transparencies**
  Studio designed for a professional presentation – no fuss, no poor handwriting, no spelling mistakes!
- **Photocopiable Handouts**
  Summaries of all the main points for your group to take away.
  No need to write notes, accuracy guaranteed.

Plus
- **£100 OFF WHEN YOU PURCHASE A SELECTED VIDEO FROM LONGMAN TRAINING!**

Tick the box overleaf for more information on the Ready Made Activities Resource Packs

----

Free Information Service
Pitman Professional Publishing
FREEPOST
128 Long Acre
LONDON
WC2E 9BR, UK

**No stamp
necessary
in the UK**

Ready made activities for
CUSTOMER CARE

The Institute of Management (IM) is at the forefront of management development and best management practice. The Institute embraces all levels of management from students to chief executives. It provides a unique portfolio of services for all managers, enabling them to develop skills and achieve management excellence. If you would like to hear more about the benefits of membership, please write to Department P, Institute of Management, Cottingham Road, Corby NN17 1TT. This series is commissioned by the Institute of Management Foundation.

Ready made activities for CUSTOMER CARE

Simon Johnson

the Institute
of Management

FOUNDATION

PITMAN
PUBLISHING

PITMAN PUBLISHING
128 Long Acre, London WC2E 9AN

A Division of Longman Group Limited

First published in Great Britain 1994

British Library Cataloguing in Publication Data
A CIP catalogue record for this book can be obtained from the British Library.

ISBN 0 273 60684 0

10 9 8 7 6 5 4 3 2 1

Typeset by PanTek Arts, Maidstone, Kent.
Printed and bound in Great Britain by Clays Ltd, St Ives plc.

The Publishers' policy is to use paper manufactured from sustainable forests.

Contents

Acknowledgements

Many people have assisted me in bringing this book to fruition, but in particular, I would like to thank David Crosby and the team at Pitman Publishing for their help and encouragement. The many people who have attended customer care courses, acted out the role plays and provided so much of the everyday evidence of customer behaviour.

My daughter, Pippa, for reading and correcting the manuscript, and to James Tansley for the line drawings. My sincere thanks go to Sylvia Thorpe for all her word processing skills and being able to interpret my handwriting, and, as always, to my wife, Anne, for her total support and her encouragement to do it.

Introduction

The subject of customer care, or service, has been a major item in training calendars for some time.

Most training companies and consultancies run or offer programmes, and most of the major service industry firms include a form of customer care training, either at induction or at some time during the early weeks after new members of staff join them. These programmes vary from a one-day appreciation to what can only be described as 'happy clappy' events or campaigns that seek to instil company loyalties and a system of procedures and staff behaviour to ensure that friendly care is given.

The dangers of such programmes are that they are often only 'skin deep'; little is learned other than some catchphrases and basic activities and, unless constant and expensive updating is maintained, the effect soon fades. Furthermore, in service companies, there is a reliance on part-time labour, many staff move on to other jobs, and, when a business crisis looms or training becomes expensive, any customer care activities tend to be abandoned.

This book seeks to address and prevent such problems. It provides, within its eight chapters, some down-to-earth advice for management and staff on how to launch, control, and update a customer care approach. Then, at the end of each chapter, a series of training and operational tasks and exercises are suggested that will ensure that customer care and service are retained at the forefront of any company wanting to keep its customers happy and provide them with value for money.

This unique approach coincides with the more concerted effort by Government and its training agencies to provide National Vocational Qualifications for a large percentage of the workforce, whatever a person's age or academic ability. To this end, there is now a National Vocational Qualification (NVQ) in customer service – launched in 1994 by the Customer Service Lead Body. The competence-based standards have been developed:

> *'for those organizations whose corporate strategy genuinely centres around creating delighted customers.'*

The Lead Body goes on to state that:

'in developing the standards [they] quickly identified that to be minimally competent at customer service, individuals needed a mature approach, coupled with experience and a strategic understanding of the formal and informal systems of their organization. The Award is therefore targeted at Level 3.'

This level equates with a supervisor grade in an organization and is therefore a useful target to aim for in developing and assessing customer care training.

The five units of the Award are:

- maintain reliable customer service
- communicate with customers
- develop positive working relationships with customers
- solve problems on behalf of customers
- initiate and evaluate change to improve service to customers.

The essence of any NVQ is that evidence of competence in a given task is obtained by actually performing it. This performance is best assessed by a person's supervisor over a period of time in their normal place of work.

This book, therefore, will serve as a useful support to the achievement of an NVQ in customer service.

The eight chapters cover the following.

- *An overview of care* Sets out why customer care is important and how management can introduce and monitor an effective service and care training programme. The training section concentrates on the vital induction period and the importance of job knowledge and teamwork.

- *The process of care* Explains how every customer 'looks forward' to the service experience and how staff can meet these expectations by creating the right first and last impression on the customer. The training section concentrates on this welcoming process and suggests a number of operational activities that will enhance the welcome or farewell.

- *Selling care* Looks at the added extras that are often forgotten when serving customers. The expertise, professionalism, and reliability of the person as well as the product are of vital importance. The training required to support this end is then outlined.

- *Standards and quality* Concentrates on how, by setting effective service and care standards, the quality element – so important in business today – can be monitored and constantly improved (the training exercises here fit neatly with Unit 5 of the NVQ).

- *Skills and competencies* Those needed by staff to provide the best customer care are looked at in some detail, drawing on recent research carried out in America and Europe. The training element supports this by suggesting ways in which each skill or competence can be 'trained in'.

- *How or why things go wrong* The problems of complaints, difficult customers, making assumptions, and overcoming prejudice are discussed in two chapters. Attitude, approach, and appearance are also covered, as are telephone techniques and after-sales issues.

- *The manager's and supervisor's role* How this involves overseeing and being part of the care process. The chapter concludes with a check-list of questions to ensure that care training and procedures are kept under review.

Although there can be no substitute for real-life experiences when organizing case studies or role plays, the book concludes with a number to supplement everyday examples. Those using them are invited to draw up their own lessons and conclusions.

In summary, the book seeks to achieve the following:

- an all-in-one explanation of how a customer care programme should be introduced, with relevant training activities

- a stepping into the 'customer's shoes' explanation of the process of expectation

- a practical link to the achievement of an NVQ in customer service, assessed in the workplace by managers and supervisors

- an explanation, with training back-up, as to the skills, competencies and tasks needed to maintain effective customer care and how to handle any difficulties that may arise

- easy-to-use training activities and exercises that can be handled effectively by unqualified trainers

- handy case study and role play examples

- a means whereby a continuous review of customer care can be achieved.

The whole is written in an easy-to-read way so that it is accessible to all.

1

AN OVERVIEW OF CARE

INTRODUCTION

Over the years, in both service and manufacturing environments, the 'bottom-line' figure has become the all-important one. While making a handsome profit for shareholders cannot be regarded as a 'bad thing', too often this has been at the customer's expense; front-line care and service taking second place to the needs of the Profit and Loss account. Money first, customer second: 'We have a Customer Service Department for them – let's get on and make savings to achieve better profits'.

To a certain extent, many customers contributed to this state of affairs. 'Customers complain with their feet' was a common remark heard in many establishments. If they were unhappy and didn't come back it didn't matter, there were plenty more!

Recessionary pressures have changed all this, with the result that it is now vital not only to entice new or existing customers back to a company, but also to hold on to them by offering inducements, discounts, special offers, even to care for them! In effect, becoming a customer-led company.

Furthermore, we are moving away from the automatic catchphrase – the 'have a nice day' syndrome – to instilling a genuine desire to care. No longer an automatic empty smile, but, rather, a will to understand the customer's needs and wants by the person in contact. A feeling that it really *does* matter how we treat or care for the customers, because they are keeping the business alive.

WHAT IS CARE?

This book, including the training exercises at the end of each chapter, seeks to answer this question. To serve as an introduction to the word, the dictionary defines care as, among other meanings, 'showing concern and interest'. Extending this into a business environment, we can interpret this as training for, or preferably a natural desire by, the server or provider to go out of their way to meet their customer's needs. It suggests the need to seek out, by careful and natural questions (not a formal check-list), what the customer wants *exactly*, and then do all that is possible to meet their wants. Furthermore, it has to be *the same standard of care* however small the request, and, equally important, the same standard, however difficult the customer.

It is very important that the company has its own definition of customer care, known by everyone, in order to ensure a common standard throughout the organization.

WHAT IT MEANS?

For any company, large or small, providing the best care has to involve every single aspect of customer contact.

It should encompass recruitment procedures, to ensure that contact staff are properly selected for their care expertise, in addition to the necessary skills for the job. These staff should also be acceptable to the customers who are attracted to the company through sales and marketing campaigns.

It means holding an effective and thorough induction programme, that not only gives new employees details of the company, legislation, and departmental procedures, but also 'trains in' its care policy and ensures, through role plays and observation on the job, that new staff members can provide the necessary care. Training exercises that help in this are on page 9.

This training (and observation) should be followed up regularly by the Manager or Head of Department to maintain the principle of care, correct any shortcomings or introduce new methods. Managers and supervisors are not to be excepted; in addition to maintaining a check-list of care, they, too, have to receive regular refreshers so that *every* level of contact is continually covered.

Above all, care means instilling two important words into the everyday working lives of those in contact with customers – and those who are not. These words are *belonging* and *belief*. By 'belonging' I mean being part of a team or company that cares about its staff, its product, and customers. Those providing the care have to be made to feel part of a successful team, even a family, where they learn the value of belonging to the team as well as understanding what can happen if they let the team down, how care can suffer. Belonging leads to an understanding of the second word. Staff need to have 'belief' in a number of things: the company, the products, the team, the person, and the customers.

SERVICE PLUS CARE – THE ADDED INGREDIENT

Providing a service but paying only lip-service to care often means producing something quickly according to the rules; the required number of customers through a checkout each hour, the turn-round in a fast-food restaurant, the speed of response to a telephone call.

Such rules often add to the misery – an automatic message delivered in a bored voice, excessive use of the customer's name (because that's the rule) – and the result is that the customer feels like a number or just another item on a conveyor belt.

When care is added to the rules it does not prevent the system operating successfully, but, rather, provides the personal touch – the genuine smile, having the time (or at least finding those extra seconds) to make the customer feel like a person again, feel valued for being there. Achieving this is simple, just turn the tables round and examine how you would feel as a customer if the rules and procedures were applied to you.

Adding care should *not* result in an 'over the top' dramatic performance. By providing too much care, the customer can feel embarrassed, even annoyed at having to answer too many questions. It is not necessary to find out a person's life history and future plans to travel overseas just because they want to buy a shortwave radio or to overdo the praise because they choose a particular dish on the menu.

This added ingredient requires staff to 'read the customer' and provide just the right amount of care and attention (that which they *need*) at a given moment. What they need can easily alter. For example, hotel residents are often totally different in their care needs at lunch and dinner. So, too, are customers on the telephone compared to those you deal with face-to-face.

TOP TO BOTTOM CARE

A simple question to ask of anyone in a service environment is: 'In one word, who are your customers?' The answer is *'Everyone!'*

Everyone is *someone's* customer. They may not be paying customers, but they have a right to be cared for. The meter reader, delivery driver, maintenance engineer, police officer, even one's own personal friends can be your customers. They will know something of your business, you of theirs; it is important to treat everyone with the care they deserve. The benefits to your business could be enormous for people you least expect to provide many sales opportunities for you over a period of time: 'While reading the meter at the Dog and Duck they looked after me so well. Lovely menu, you should go and try it some time'!

The other side of this coin, of course, is that every member of *staff* is a customer of yours as well. They *also* require care. Moreover, it has to be remembered that *every* member of a team has some responsibility for the care of customers, even if they are not in direct contact with them. It came as a great shock to many hotel chefs some years ago when they had to leave their kitchens and operate a carvery – actually talking to diners. No longer could they hide behind the 'hotplate barrier' and leave the waiting staff to cope with any complaints about their cooking.

So often, too, management overlook the members of staff who can really make all the difference to the image of the company. Two such examples are table clearers in a self-service restaurant and service engineers for an electrical company. Both have far more time and opportunity than the managers to sell the company during their direct contact with the customers. All, therefore, should be involved in care training .

THE MANAGER'S ROLE

Today most of the initiatives urged on companies require a full and determined commitment from the top. Investors in People and BS5750 being two such examples. Care is no exception. It makes no sense for a staff member in contact with customers and offering the best care to be undermined by head-office or top-management bureaucracy.

Caring for the customer is part of a leader's role and must be passed right down the organization. Care is part of everyone's job role or work schedule, backed up by effective training at induction and thereafter at regular intervals.

One way of building this into management practice is to remember the acronym, CICC, which stands for the elements essential to ensuring that care works:

C = *consultation* talk to people, staff, customers about the sort of care that should be provided to bring about

I = *involvement* by everyone in the need to put customers first and their role in the policy of caring to bring about

C = *commitment* to actually carrying out the policy and making it work at every level

C = *communication* policies, procedures, standards are laid down in writing so that checks can be made against these standards, and amendments agreed should certain elements not work.

Care, therefore, has to be at the forefront in service procedures and be known by everyone – even if this means printing it at the top of every noticeboard.

MEASURING CARE

Talk of standards brings us neatly to the topic of measuring care, another important task with CICC-style management. It is essential to:

- establish what customers actually want
- decide how the standard of care is perceived now
- work out what gaps need to be filled.

This results in a need for training to fill the gaps not just to fit the care to what the customers actually want, but to provide levels of service and care that better these. Then, operational standards and procedures for making it work need to be set.

These standards are then communicated and, once added to the face-to-face training activity, provide the foundations for the policy. Take care not to make each standard too prescriptive, though. Just bear in mind how offputting it is to listen to a bored telephonist trotting out the message: 'XYZ Co., Sam speaking, sorry to have kept you, how may I help?'

CUSTOMER CARE = STAFF CARE

Finally, it is important for managers to realize that really good customer care comes only by providing good staff care. Uniforms, changing facilities, clubs, discounts are some areas to be considered and added to the traditional good pay, pensions, eating facilities, and welfare. What is required is for contact staff to enjoy coming to work and being part of a team; feeling comfortable with their appearance, being able to think and act for themselves (within the limits agreed), and not living in fear of management clampdowns.

Ultimately, pride in the job generates happiness and contentment, which shows through in a relaxed and efficient approach to customer care.

This, then, is our overview. Some training activities now follow.

Training activities

1 INDUCTION

As pointed out on page 4, good customer care starts with an effective induction programme provided by a trainer, or the various heads of department.

Such a programme should include:

● legal requirements – health, safety, fire, sickness
● company personalities – Chairman, directors, managers
● tour of the building or site – to gain an overall idea of the company
● procedures, rules, and regulations – discipline, grievance, uniform
● product knowledge and standards.

It is also valuable to include the company's own definition of customer care – you may like to give details of some of the regular customers. The overall objective is to create *belief* in the products and the company, and to build up the equation

Good staff care = good customer care.

For an example of a check-list that could be used to ensure that all these areas are covered, during induction, see Figure 1.1. The kinds of information staff need to know are outlined below the headings but, of course, you will need to choose items that are appropriate to your enterprise.

2 TURNING CUSTOMERS INTO STAFF

Before joining a company, new staff were potential or actual customers of that company. Now, they are on the other side of the counter, as it were, and have to present the company line to the customers. The training is aimed at finding out what they (as customers) thought of the company – either as a genuine customer or through first impressions. So:

● probe regarding their first contact with the company – what form it took, whether it was a visit, telephone call, letter, advertisement

Figure 1.1 Example of a check-list to be filled in as each area is covered during the induction of new staff

SECTION 1: THE ESTABLISHMENT		
Task	*Completed/Date*	*Comments*
Staff handbook issued **A The company** Background and history, size, branches, other companies in group, reputation and product range.		
B The building History and background. Means of entry, safety rules. Tour of building to show all areas.		
C The industry Size and importance of .... (say, retail) business. (How many employed, exports, local economy and so on.) Where company fits into the overall pattern of the industry.		
D Personalities Senior company and local management personnel. Individual supervisors, personnel, staff, and so on.		
E Legislation Health and safety, fire procedures (link to building tour), hygiene factors, working practices, reporting sick, looking after/using equipment, procedures in event of an accident, and use of energy/conservation.		
F Personal Welfare arrangements, hours of work, overtime procedure, pay producedure/sick pay, holiday entitlement, discipline and grievance, contracts, union membership, discounts, privileges, incentives, and so on.		

Figure 1.1 cont'd

Task	Completed/Date	Comments
G Uniform Fitting and care, cleaning and replacement.		
H Planning and teamwork The job, tasks and procedures, planning, timekeeping, preparing the area, working with others, recognizing authority, liaising with other departments, becoming a team member, and so on.		
I Customers Who they are, what they want.		

Note regarding overal care policy

Once induction has been completed, the new member of staff can commence the care training. It is important to devise a series of test questions to ensure that there has been a complete understanding of all of the above.

● find out how well they were treated or received – get honest answers

● arriving at the company for the first time, what impression they formed of it – from the outside of the buildings, the car park, reception, signs, gardens, and so on.

It is important to try and prompt new staff to be as open and honest as possible. Take notes and follow up any problems you identify.

3 BASIC CARE TRAINING

The induction training and interviews will have brought out the basic reasons for the company's existence, its policies and objectives. This basic care training can be carried out as part of the induction process or by the section heads as new employees start work.

First, establish who the customers are

As we have seen, the real answer is *everyone* – staff, delivery drivers, post-men and women, maintenance, utilities, and, of course, the *customers*.

It is important to stress that staff are ambassadors of the company, both inside and out. Meeting friends, family, casual contacts – all are opportunities to pro-mote the company.

Second, what do they want?

A simple question with some simple answers: service, satisfaction, value for money. They also want care, attention, expertise (help), friendliness, good manners, and much more.

Third, why do customers come to the company?

The answers expected here are reputation, the products and service, the staff.

The answers to these three questions should be recorded and will provide the basic essentials of customer care training. In summary, everyone is a cus-tomer of someone else, so that even if they are not in direct contact with customers, staff are contributing to the success of the company when they are ambassadors for it who believe in their job, their company, and themselves.

Definitions

To get further commitment to customer care from new staff, ask the simple question: 'What to you is customer care?' Can they suggest better ways to effect this than those already being used in the company?

Answers should include: good service, friendliness, efficiency, product know-ledge, knowing the customers, a genuine smile, meeting/exceeding demands.

Some definitions

- Always meeting our customers' basic expectations.
- The same welcome and service everywhere.
- The same good care however small is the request or difficult the customer.
- Consistently meeting or exceeding customer needs or requirements.
- Ensuring that the customer feels valued and understood.

Figure 1.2 Example of check-list for basic care training

SECTION 3: BASIC CARE TRAINING		
Task	*Completed/Date*	*Comments*
A The customers Who our customers are, where they come from, how they were attracted to us, what they expect, definition of company care, the staff's role as ambassadors, putting across the care image, and maintaining the reputation.		
B Basic procedures Correct uniform, wearing badges, and so on, the welcome, greeting, practise role plays, knowing the product, selling the product, knowing names, customers/managers, other relevant staff, the team (who can help in certain situations), telephone answering procedure, using equipment (tills, and so on) while in customer's presence, the farewell, record keeping, and building up personal memory.		
C Personal care policy Attitude, mood, preparedness, aware of needs, avoiding stress, looking at job through customer's eyes, reporting problems, complaints procedures, and being a team member.		

Note

The above tasks are guidelines only, and for use with staff. As confidence and knowledge grows, more tasks will be given and more contract with customers expected.

This check-list is also useful when carrying out routine departmental checks or updating training sessions.

What is expected of new staff in customer care

This final section underlines the whole care process by laying down, from day one, what staff have to do to maintain care. In addition to the expected requirements of arriving on time, being awake, and meeting all the customer needs suggested above, staff should be reminded about:

- *their uniform* that when they wear it, they are representing the company and so take care of their appearance
- *their mood* that when dealing with customers, they are on stage, performing, so moods have to be left behind; they should never react to a customer or let them get them down
- *stress* that they should keep it at bay by concentrating on the job, not on their own troubles, and by talking over problems with others – handling people can be hard work
- *knowing the job and the product* that they should build up knowledge of the job quickly so that customers can be handled and cared for easily
- *awareness* that they should always be ready for customers, not caught out, and above all, know the regulars.

In summary, enjoy the work, and believe in yourself, the company, and the product. Remember two important phrases:

- put yourself in your customer's shoes
- ask 'Would I be happy with my service if I was my customer?'

For an example of a check-list of the kinds of tasks new staff could be asked to do during their basic care training, see Figure 1.2. Figure 1.3 is a check-list each member of staff can use all the time.

4 MANAGEMENT TASKS

To stress the overview of customer care, practise the CICC principle – involve, and, therefore, commit, all management to the care ethic, and ensure that this policy is properly communicated throughout the organization.

Figure 1.3 Staff check-list: caring for customers

PERSONAL CUSTOMER CARE

Do I . . .

arrive on time?

know and sell the products?

know and help my team?

put personal problems aside?

know regular customers by name?

wear my uniform and badge correctly and proudly?

care for myself, my health, and appearance?

show a genuine desire to help my customers?

work cheerfully?

give a warm welcome/final farewell in my voice
    (face-to-face or on the telephone)?

always greet customers quickly and confidently?

know the company/department's basic care standards?

keep the workplace neat and tidy?

know how to use the equipment in view of the customers?

look at the whole area regularly for neatness and tidiness?

give of my best throughout my shift?

never let the company down inside or outside work?

always assist customers?

know all of my job?

put myself in my customer's shoes to check my care of them?

would I be happy with my performance if I were my customer?

As a final check on the induction process, it is suggested that staff are given a card along the above lines to keep with them as they work as their own personal care check-list.

Figure 1.4 Management check-list: customer contact

SECTION 4: MANAGEMENT TASKS		
Aspects of contact with company	*Company staff involved*	*Comments*
A Personal Out-of-hours contact, social/sports, and so on.		
B Advertisements Personnel, products, promotions, press, radio, TV.		
C Customer to customer Reputation, message, product performance, and so on.		
D Outside areas Car park, grounds, entrance lobbies, loading bay, delivery areas, and so on.		
E First contact Reception, telephone call, written promotional material, letters to staff/customers, reply letters, and so on.		
F General contact All front-line staff, all support staff, service counters, sales teams and so on.		

Note

The above check-list shows the areas managers should look at and gives some suggestions as to what types of contact fall under these headings. The final list can be quite considerable. By completing both columns, it will be possible to list the main company personnel involved in the various types of contact and what elements of care are involved. The most important column is the 'Comments' column. Here managers should answer the question posed about how contact is made, what happens, and so on. From all this information, problem areas are easily identified and the staff involved can be targeted for specific care training.

Some ways of achieving this include the following.

● Require the team to list *all* the areas within and outside the company where customer contact occurs, saying:
  – how is this contact made
  – what happens
  – whether or not it complies with the care policy
  – whether or not it is entirely satisfactory
  – make suggestions for change and improvement with reasons and plans.

● Report on how care is perceived by these customers, again suggesting changes or improvements.

● Then, have the managers look at the company from the customer's point of view (as during the induction process, look at the welcome received, outside areas, literature, telephone answering, first and last impressions, and so on). Again, produce a report with reasoned changes or improvements (see Figure 1.4).

● For the specialized departments, such as personnel, training, and sales, some further tasks are highlighted (see Figure 1.5).

The following is a useful check-list for specialist staff whose task is to ensure that regular training in caring for customers is maintained and updated.

Figure 1.5 Check-list for personnel and training departments

SECTION 4: MANAGEMENT TASKS		
Training activity	*(Date) Completed on/by*	*Comments*
1 New induction programme run for month of		
2 Staff handbooks issued.		
3 New staff passed to .... Department .... Department .... Department		
4 Departmental training record received from		

Figure 1.5 Cont'd

Training activity	(Date) Completed on/by	Comments

5 Update care training sessions
    completed in
    .... Department
    .... Department		

6 New care policy issued.		

7 New training course actioned:
    • general
    • .... Department
    • .... Department		

8 Spot review of care training
    undertaken in
    .... Department
    .... Department		

9 Customer survey undertaken.		
10 New training course actioned.		

Note

The above check-list shows the areas managers should look at and give some suggestions as to what types of contact fall under these headings. The final list can be quite considerable. By completing all three columns, it will be possible to list the main company personnel involved in the various types of contact and what elements of care are involved. The most important column is the 'Comments' column. Here managers should answer the question posed about how contact is made, what happens, and so on. From all this information, problem areas are easily identified and the staff involved can be targeted for specific care training.

- Check on departmental training programmes (following the new care-biased induction process). How much attention is paid to customer care?

- Institute regular updating sessions, to keep care in the forefront of training activities.

- Assess how advertising and recruitment of staff links to the sales and marketing of the products and, therefore, to attracting certain types of customers for those products. Is there common ground? Can the staff understand the customer? What training is required?

- How do the advertisements for staff and products reflect the care policy? (See Figure 1.6.)

Advertisement A

The XYZ Hotel requires

Shift Receptionist to work in our busy computerized office.
We pride ourselves on the welcome and care we provide for all our guests
and visitors. We therefore are looking for staff who will be cheerful, personable, and
caring. Good training provided. Attractive uniform.
We genuinely care for our staff.

Write or telephone Mr .... for an appointment to talk over your application.

Advertisement B

The XYZ Hotel requires

Shift Receptionist for busy commercial hotel.
Two years' experience in similar capacity needed.
Full training in the use of our modern computer provided.

For application form contact ....

Perhaps a very exaggerated case, but although Advertisement A will cost considerably more to place, the standard of the applicants is likely to be much higher than those for Advertisement B, even though they may *not* have two years' experience. The genuine caring attitude of the first comes across.

Figure 1.6 Reflecting your care policy in company recruitment advertising

2

··

THE PROCESS OF CARE – ACHIEVING THE RIGHT IMPRESSION

THE PROBLEM

In Chapter 1 and in the accompanying training activities, we have seen that there is a need to foster care (of customers and staff) right from the top to the bottom of any organization. This begins at the induction stage and continues within every department through regular training sessions and checks on how well care is being achieved against standards, that are laid down.

This puts pressure on every manager and supervisor to not only know what these standards are – and have a hand in both setting and reviewing them – but also to constantly oversee how well their staff are practising them, correcting the problems, and praising good performance.

Care has to be seen to happen throughout an organization. Unfortunately, in many, it only occurs in small pockets, where a specific member of staff takes it upon themselves to put the customer first. So often, this initiative is not supported by the 'system' and the staff member becomes frustrated and leaves.

Others blame the system for the lack of care, saying, for example, 'Our computer run is next week, we can't do anything until then'.

HOW TO PUT IT RIGHT

There are four main solutions to this situation:

- a communications care map
- establishing priorities
- examining customer processes
- creating and leaving an impression.

Let us examine each of these in turn.

The communications care map

Despite the fact that today we probably have hundreds of ways of communicating – faxes, satellites, video, telephones – we still regularly hear the cry 'communications are terrible'. In theory, information should travel up, down, and across an organization in ways that mean everyone can understand the message, but how often does this really happen? A communications map should show how messages are relayed, where and when meetings occur, and who interrelates with whom.

A care map works in a similar way. Remembering that everyone is a customer of someone else, both inside and outside an organization, the map should show:

- who relies on whom for information
- who relates to whom about what
- how the information reaches the 'sharp end', and gets back again
- how the care process moves across the company.

The map should clearly show the relationships between departments and branches (even when they are in different countries) and, most significantly, the main contact points with customers. Thus, the map can identify who has a hand in meeting customer needs and where things might go wrong. It will identify the priority areas for care.

Establishing priorities

These priority areas are principally where staff and customers meet or communicate. In military terms, these are as follows.

- *The 'front line'* This is our first priority area. This can be the parts counter at the garage, the reception desk at the office or hotel, the tills at the store or supermarket, but it is also the office that deals with the correspondence, the telephone exchange or the goods inwards bay. Specific forms of training need to be focused on these areas.

- *The impression area* This is the second priority area and, as has been discussed, care is not entirely about people talking to people; it also embraces the impression given by the 'ambience' of the establishment before a word has been spoken. These 'abstract' areas include the car park, the state of the building, paintwork, litter, frequency of grass cutting, even how clean the windows are, and, particularly, how clean the toilets are! It also includes the advertising – both for the goods, products, and promotions and also for staff vacancies.

Giving the right impression is all important because it tells the customer how efficient the company is, how much it cares. It also makes the job of the first contact person that much easier.

As well as the *first* impression, the *last* impression is equally, if not more, important. Although the majority view is again the outside areas of the building – the final impression being the first thing remembered – care has to be displayed in any leaflets or other written material given for the customer to read later. Of particular importance, of course, is the impression staff leave the customers with as they go – not an automatic mumbling of 'Have a nice day', but a genuine feeling of being sorry that they are going. This can be backed up by useful information or give-aways. Some examples include advice on avoiding local roadworks or commenting on the weather reports. One company, a farm/guest accommodation establishment in the West Country provides half-a-dozen new-laid eggs as a farewell present – this has resulted in a huge list of regular guests!

The final impression area is the interdepartmental reliance system.

- *Interdepartmental reliance system* Our care map, if compiled correctly, should have identified the 'flow chart' of customer care across departments or branches of the company and, therefore, where systems can break down. For example, the effect of the warehouse not sending out the goods promised by the retail sector or the accounts office not settling an invoice within the terms agreed by sales.

We have all suffered from the telephone buck passing experience and the effect this can have on our view of an otherwise efficient company. How much better, then, to consider care when setting up and managing the flow of paperwork and information, even to the extent of enabling the person taking the call to have the authority to deal with the query completely by themselves!

Customer processes

'I am really looking forward to the weekend.' This statement is probably made many times by thousands of people every Monday morning! But what does it actually mean? Life is a mixture of looking back on our experiences and looking forwards, either with pleasure or dread, to the short- or long-term future. Let's look at our expectant weekender. They have made a booking for a lazy weekend in the country, which has meant already contacting, and hopefully being well received by, an hotelier, who has an efficient booking system and well-trained reception and other staff.

Figure 2.1 The 'looking forward to' feeling can quickly be submerged by negative experiences on the way

Thus, the anticipation has begun, where Friday night comes to be seen as the high point of a dull week. However, on Friday, travel or weather problems may cause all sorts of difficulties so that by the time the hotel is reached, the 'looking forward to' feeling has become a *'why* did we bother?' feeling (see Figure 2.1). This is when the care process has to go into overdrive so that the now plummeting line on the expectation graph is quickly routed back upwards again so that the 'knockdown' of the motorway delays, cancelled train, flat tyre or whatever is rapidly forgotten.

This requires, in addition to personal care, providing the unexpected: the special late meal, the free drink, and being ready for unusual requests; knowing the name of the local garage or other means of effecting a repair, providing an alternative route home to miss the roadworks. There are many ways of surprising the customers – again establishing that vital positive last impression.

It is these sorts of small pieces of inexpensive but extra care that single out the best companies and create or leave the right impression.

Creating or leaving the right impression

This is best achieved by, again, recognizing the fundamental message of putting yourself in your customer's shoes. Look at the operation being provided through the eyes of your customers – how would you feel if it happened to you, what would you expect? In the case of our weekender, it is more than words of sympathy!

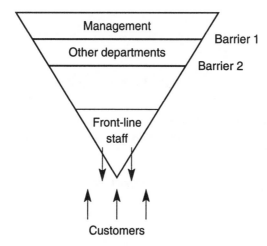

Figure 2.2 How front-line staff come to provide care without back up

A key to the process of care and the impression we need to leave with our customers, is the word *teamwork*. So often, the sharp end of care is left to a small group of staff who are working without back-up or an effective communication system.

As Figure 2.2 shows, barriers often build up between the front-line staff and back-up departments, and, more importantly, between them and management, who are 'too busy to be involved in caring for customers'. However, all these people are part of the *team* and have some involvement in creating or leaving the right impression.

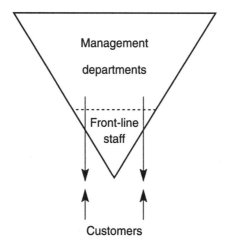

Figure 2.3 The improved situation of the 'open triangle' where front-line staff receive adequate back-up

What has to be achieved is the 'open triangle' shown in Figure 2.3. Here there is open communication – no barriers – and a back-up system so that front-line staff can be confident of effective support.

Ultimately, the triangle should be reversed (see Figure 2.4) with a much broader 'front' meeting the incoming customers. Within the team, everyone knows what has to be done, speaks with the same authority, and knows the effect the right impressions will leave with the customers.

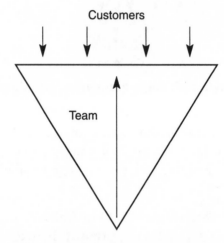

Figure 2.4 The ideal of the reversed triangle with everyone working as a team in the care of customers

Training activities

· ·

These are divided into management tasks and front-line staff specialist training.

1 MANAGEMENT

The first task is to get the management team to construct a communications care map, which has to show *all* the relationships between branches, departments or sections and the main customer contact points (for an example, see Figure 2.5). It must answer all the following questions.

● Who relies on whom for customer information?

● Who relates to whom regarding customer orders, requests, and so on?

● What is the normal information required – is it of the right standard?

● How does this information come from the customer to the end point and back again? (Forms of communication.)

● Where are the blockages or gaps and how can they be cleared or filled?

Figure 2.5 A simple example of a communications care map – 'follow the parcel'

1 **Manufacturer produces new product**
   Circulates information to *retail company*
   Sales Manager in contact with *Manager*.
   Manager in contact with *Advertising Manager*.
   Manager in contact with *advertising agency*.

2 **Advertisment produced**
   Advertising agency in contact with *retail company*.
   Retail company circulates information to *all staff*.
   Product knowledge training sessions begin.

3 **Customer sees advertisement – decides to buy.**
   Telephones order or visits *retail outlet*.
   Customer in contact with *knowledgeable staff* member.
   Sees shop model – places order.

Figure 2.5 Cont'd

4 **Shop places order with wholesaler**
Retailer's order office in contact with *wholesaler's order office*.
Wholesaler's order office in contact with *manufacturer*.

5 **Manufacturer sends goods to wholesaler**
Delivery driver in contact with *despatch*.
Delivery driver in contact with *goods inwards*.
Wholesaler sends goods to *retailer's warehouse*.
Wholesaler's delivery driver in contact as above.

6 **Warehouse contacts retail outlet – goods have arrived**
Warehouse office in contact with order office/retail outlet
Retail outlet contacts *customer*.
Retail outlet contacts *departmental Manager/staff*.
Departmental Manager in contact with *Accounts office*
    regarding payment method.
All staff aware of customer's need.

7 **Customer collects**
Contact with *retail outlet staff*.
Contact with *Accounts staff*. Makes payment.

8 **The follow-up**
Customer Service checks on/receives feedback on product.
Passes back to *manufacturers*.

Note

This map shows eight main contact points, and many human contact points within these, as the 'parcel' is followed. It is now easy to see where delays or difficulties could occur, why it can take so long for even a simple order to be processed, and how customer care can suffer if the process does not operate smoothly. It also shows how, at each stage or contact point, 'customers' have to be cared for.

Once completed the map should show the problem areas.

(Figure 2.6 shows one kind of business in which the chain of processes from supplies to finished products ready for the customer would call for careful management of customer contract points.)

The second task is to produce recommendations for overcoming such problems, involving the staff in any investigation.

Figure 2.6 Imagine what main customer contact points would exist for this operation

Many of the care problems identified during the mapping process will relate to poor communications. Now, therefore, is the time to look again at how written and verbal communications operate throughout the company, with particular reference to customer care. Some useful questions to ask regarding this area could include the following.

● How are incoming telephone messages/letters/orders dealt with?

● What is the procedure for verbal customer orders/instructions?

● How do messages/replies get back to customers (length of time it takes, is it jargon-free) and who is involved?

● Are customers informed of any delays/difficulties and, if so, how, by whom, and when?

The answers to these questions will undoubtedly highlight the need for some training activity. For example, have the staff who operate the telephones also been trained in processing orders or drafting letters so that they are aware of the full picture and their role in it? And another, could the message system be speeded up by getting those who receive queries to follow them through and report back within strict time limits?

2 STAFF

The activities undertaken by management will have fully identified the front-line staff – that is, all those who are directly in contact with customers, either face-to-face, by telephone or by correspondence. These are the staff who

Figure 2.7 Extending the communications care map to reveal interdepartmental reliance

---

1 **Booking made by telephone or letter**
Received by *reservation office*, availability checked, booking accepted. *Guest* asked to confirm.
(*Problem 1* If guest forgets to confirm, but subsequently arrives, what can happen?
Problem 2 If guest fails to give any details of special requests but expects to receive them none the less (for example, because they have stayed there before and so assume hotel knows what they want) what can happen?
Problem 3 If special needs are requested but not recorded what can happen?

2 **Guest confirms booking**
Received by *reservation office*. Booking procedure completed. Entered on specific arrival day.
(*Problem 4* If the booking procedure is not followed and the guest's name is missed off the arrival list, what can happen?)

3 **Day of arrival**
Arrival list contains room allocations and notification of special needs has been circulated to *all departments*.
(*Problem 5* If some departments do not receive the list, what can happen?
Problem 6 If vital information is left off the list, what can happen?
Problem 7 If existing guests want to stay longer, thus blocking possibility of incoming reservations, what might happen?)

4 **Guest arrives**
Registered and taken to room. *Housekeeping*, *kitchen*, *restaurant* and *other departments* notified of arrival.
(*Problem 8* If these departments are not informed (or only some are), what might happen?)

Note

Here, then, up to six different departments are reliant, first, on the original booking being properly handled, and, subsequently, each one needs to keep in touch with all the rest to ensure that the guest receives all that they require. Such an exercise brings home to many how important their individual roles are not only to their *own* departments, but to many others.

During training, have staff make a list of all those on whom they rely and to whom they have to give information. Ask them whether or not they are satisfied that it always works well.

should receive training first. They must be reminded of the training activities carried out in Chapter 1 regarding appearance, mood, stress, and so on, as well as stressing the importance of their roles as ambassadors for the company by virtue of being front-line staff.

Review with them how well the team works together, who supports whom, who they should go to for advice, and (as with the managers) where the communication and care blocks are.

It may well be that what is seen as a perfectly sound communication channel by management is viewed very differently by staff 'at the sharp end'. Be prepared to listen and act accordingly.

As an extension of the communications care map of Figure 2.5, Figure 2.7 can be used to show how reliant the staff in different departments can be on each other. The example used is that of a typical hotel booking.

Further exercise for front-line staff

Ask the staff concerned to think of as many 'rules of engagement' as they can that will help them cope with the varied needs of the customers they meet every day. For example, good communications, smiling, being confident when coping with problems.

What is required is competent performance by everyone in the team.

Once completed, you should have a list of points that cover not only the behaviour of staff towards their customers, but also some guidelines for teamwork. As a summary of the latter, here are 12 'C' words that summarize team performance:

- *clarity* be clear about the what, why, and how of a job
- *consistent* set a standard of performance, then know, stick to it or exceed it
- *context* know your place in the market, the type of service offered, and the price paid for it – make it value for money
- *colleagues* know your team, be loyal, back each other up
- *champion* know, praise, and *believe* in your products
- *communicate* tell, say, write, respond correctly to everyone who needs to know about you and your products

- *commitment* be fully involved and committed to the job, the product, customers, and members of the team
- *celebrate* when successful and when things go well
- *coalition* don't fall out – particularly in public – work together
- *consequence* know the care map and what is happening in the rest of the organization; what effect your actions will have elsewhere
- *cement* build and maintain relationships based on firm and high standards of performance and behaviour
- *courage* don't wilt under pressure, take on the job and succeed at it.

For all staff

This exercise stresses the importance of knowing the *process* of care and has three objectives:

1 to understand the process of expectation experienced by customers
2 to appreciate the importance of first impressions (and last impressions)
3 to agree how we should *welcome* our customers, and what this entails.

☞ Question

Is anyone looking forward to something at the moment? A holiday, wedding, buying something important?

Probe among the group and if no one volunteers anything, use a future holiday or an evening out, a shopping expedition or some event linked to your own company or department. (You could also use less welcome events, like a visit to the dentist or to an unpopular relation!)

If you have a volunteer, use and involve them to help the group experience 'understanding' of the situation.

To help you appreciate how this exercise works, the following example uses the build-up to a holiday.

Next summer you want to go on a UK seaside holiday, so, during the dark winter evenings you need to decide where to go. To help you what do you do?

Answers

'Ring up/visit a travel agent', 'pick up a brochure', 'look at an advertisement in a newspaper or a magazine', 'talk to a friend'.

Whatever you do, it is *the first step in the process of care*. From now on, you are 'looking forward' to the holiday. (This and the next steps can be written down in the form of a flow chart, as shown in Figure 2.8.)

The brochure or advertisement convinces you which place to choose, you have the dates in mind, so now you make contact with someone at the hotel or holiday camp of your choice or the booking agency, probably by telephone. This is the *second step* in the process. Continue to take your trainees through the process – exchange of letters, the long build-up to the holiday through the spring when the expectations are dormant but still there (I can't wait!) – the *third step*. Then comes the day of departure and the contacts experienced on the way to your destination – the *fourth step*. The first impressions of the town are the *fifth step*, then those of the site or venue and, *finally*, the personal welcome are the *sixth* and *seventh steps*.

Thus, as the holidaymaker, you could have had six contacts with people, the written word or a visual impression *before* the care of the chosen venue has started to come into play. Each one of these contacts could have soured your expectations, so the hotel receptionist could have a really big job to do to restore your mood.

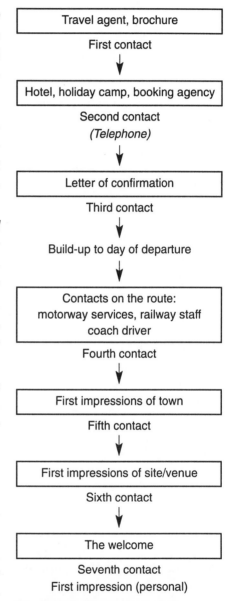

Figure 2.8 Flow chart of the customer's contacts made while booking a holiday through to beginning the holiday itself

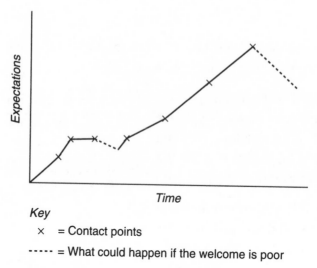

Key

× = Contact points

----- = What could happen if the welcome is poor

Figure 2.9 Expectation curve of the holidaymaker

Get your trainees to think of things that would put them in a bad mood by the time of step six. For example, long delay in answering the phone, or replying to a letter, traffic jams, overcharging at a motorway services, bad weather, train delays, a 'tatty' approach road, bad signing in a car park, poor directions, asking the 'wrong person' for directions.

To make it clearer, you can draw a graph along the lines of that shown in Figure 2.9 below the flow chart and plot the various stages in the process to produce the 'expectation curve' of the experience. This will really make it clear what happens when poor care or service is given.

It is possible to see how 'the looking forward to' feeling, the expectation of good things, can so easily be upset by something outside the control of the first person to receive them at their destination.

Question

If it is obvious that all is not right with an incoming customer, how would you treat this person as they approach you?

Some answers

1 Imagine the worst and go out of your way to be kind and welcoming (but not over the top).

2 Try to overcome any mood or leftover bad feeling that the incoming customer may still have by being attentive, asking caring questions, and ensuring satisfaction with all that *you* are doing for them.
3 Ask questions about the journey, be sympathetic, and try to assure the customer that something will be done and it's not always like this!
4 Be alert to problems – be aware of roadworks, train delays, and so on – that are likely to upset customers wanting to arrive on time.

The most important thing of all is to create the right first impression.

Two more exercises

1 Send your trainees out to a number of venues nearby – pubs, shops, hotels, car parks, anywhere serving the public (customers). Working in pairs, ask them to write down their first impression of the premises they go to (the first few minutes are the most important).
2 On their return, tell them to compare your premises or department as customers – what first impression is given? What could be improved? (Refer them back to their induction.)

List all the points raised, then consider signs, directions, ease of entry to a car park, litter, lights, cleanliness, the effect of broken equipment, paintwork, overall 'passive' welcome, and so forth. Remember, there are bound to be lessons for your own premises – use them wisely.

At the end, remind your trainees that, so far, they have not met anybody, but it is quite possible that the first impression has left the person who will be this first contact quite a lot to do.

WHAT WILL HAVE BEEN LEARNED

The messages for customer care arising from these activities are:

● always look at your own premises as if you were a *customer* receiving your *first impression* of the company
● tell someone if it doesn't match up to what is required
● look at other places (the competition) and take note of how *their* first impression strikes you
● remember, you only have a few moments (or even seconds) to make the impression and there may be no second chance.

Case studies

Here now are two short case studies that can be used to further reinforce what has been learned about the process of care and making the right impression on the customer.

THE BIRTHDAY PARTY

Mr John Sprague was a regular diner at the Bloxley House Hotel. He had lived in the area for some time, knew the Manager, Mr Masters, well, and enjoyed entertaining family and the clients of his solicitor's practice at the Hotel.

His wife's fifty-fifth birthday approached and he decided to have a big family gathering at the Hotel on the Sunday after her birthday. Children, grandchildren, relations, and family friends were invited – altogether some 30 people, including a baby and 4 children under 6 years old.

A few days before the event, Mr Sprague called at the Hotel to talk over final arrangements. Mr Masters was away at a manager's conference, but Mr Sprague had initially spoken to a receptionist who was about to go off duty. She said that the booking was fully confirmed and suggested he talked to Mrs Weston, a senior waitress, as Mr Pardini, the Restaurant Manager was away ill. This he duly did, leaving the Hotel feeling pleased that all would be well on the Sunday.

On the day in question (Mr Masters' weekend off) the Sprague party arrived and quickly discovered that all was not well at the restaurant.

Mr Pardini (now recovered) claimed to know nothing about the special vegetarian dish that had been requested for 3 people, was still assuming that only 3 children were coming (the original number), and had only laid tables for 25.

Mr Sprague's *original* wine choice (not the one he had asked for during his *last* visit) was cooling and no alternative sweet (also requested on the last visit) was available.

However, to the embarrassment of Mr Pardini, it transpired that the other kitchen staff knew all about the changes and, after some delay and hasty rearrangements, all was well. Mr Sprague contacted Mr Masters on the Monday and asked him to explain why he had been so embarrassed by the communication breakdown regarding his party.

Your task

As Mr Masters, decide who to see and what to do about the complaint. (Note that Mrs Weston now has Mr Pardini's virus and will be away for several days!)

Suggest ways in which such a problem can be avoided in the future.

Write a letter to Mr Sprague outlining the action you have taken.

THE GARAGE RECEPTIONIST

Jenny Smith has always been keen on cars and engines. After taking a business studies course at college, she manages to obtain a job at the reception desk of a local popular garage, dealing with servicing and repairs.

The garage has a sophisticated computer system, installed by a major car manufacturer, that maintains a database of information regarding regular customer's cars. This week, the garage's owner is away at a dealer's conference and the Service Manager is on an updating course.

Most of the mechanics rather resent Jenny – not publicly, but they are not keen to help (the son of one of them had been turned down for her job). Jenny's training (this is her second week) has rather been left to chance, so problems start to build up as the week progresses.

On Friday, she is late for work because her bus was cancelled and she arrives to find six angry drivers waiting to book their cars in. No one in the service bay has covered for her.

After these customers have been seen to, things calm down and Jenny can try to catch up. To her horror, she discovers that the computer has malfunctioned and therefore there is a strong possibility that the wrong instructions have been passed to the mechanics about several cars.

Worse is to follow. At 5.00 pm, Mr Jonas, a local company director returns to collect his car before going on holiday to discover that it has not been touched, despite the fact that he told Jenny how urgent the repair was!

Mr Jonas has a quick temper and is in full flow when the garage's owner returns from his conference.

Your task

As the owner of the garage, decide:

● what you have to do immediately
● what has gone wrong
● what should have happened when Jenny first joined
● what should now be done to ensure that it doesn't happen again.

Tutor's notes

In both case studies, there has been a problem with communication.

In the hotel, one department *has* received the information, but another *hasn't*, resulting in embarrassment for the customer. Some system for updating party information has to be actioned, and any staff who take messages from guests need to be trained how to use it. Also, consider the role and responsibility of the receptionist; she went off duty without ensuring that Mr Sprague had been properly attended to.

At the garage there is a lack of training for this front-line member of staff, resentment, too many senior people away at once, computer failure (either human or mechanical), and, perhaps, just plain bad luck that the bus cancellation set off a chain reaction.

In both cases, steer your trainees towards a solution that highlights the need for good training of front-line staff and the importance of teamwork.

☞ Role plays

At the end of training, you might want to use a few role plays to bring home what the care process is about. Here are some specific examples of what you could do.

1 Play out the roles of Mr Masters and Mr Sprague in the previous two case studies. First have Mr Sprague ring up to speak to Mr Masters about the problem. Then, once a group solution has been found, have Mr Masters ringing up Mr Sprague to apologize.

2 Take the role of the owner of the garage in the scenario set out in the second case study. He has just walked in to discover an angry scene – a

distraught Jenny, an enraged man, threatening all sorts of retribution. The task, to quickly calm down all parties, carry out damage limitation, and have Mr Jonas' car sorted out.

3 You are a customer and you have ordered a blue lounge suite from your local department store. There is a six-week delivery lead, so you ask for it to be sent to you as soon as it arrives in the shop.

You are telephoned by the Furniture Department of the store to say that your suite has arrived and will be delivered on Monday.

It has just been placed in your lounge, and you discover that it is the wrong colour. Furious, you immediately ring the department store.

You are the Manager of the Furniture Department and have been called to the phone to deal with this irate customer who has just had a lounge suite delivered by your shop. Apparently it is the wrong colour.

4 You are walking from one village to the next while on holiday. Feeling thirsty you call into a local pub on the way. It looks quite welcoming, it has a neat garden, tidy car park, and so on. However, on going into the toilet, you discover a different story. It is smelly, dirty, and there is no paper. You go into the bar to complain.

You are a member of staff behind the bar in this pub. The tenants are out and business is quiet. You have prepared the bar and restocked the shelves and now await the first customer. This customer, coming from the direction of the toilet, seems rather upset.

3

···

ACHIEVING A WELCOME – SELLING CARE

MOVING FROM PASSIVE TO ACTIVE CARE

In Chapter 2 we looked at ensuring that the first and last impressions we make on our customers are the right ones by means of *passive* care – the cleanliness of the outside of the premises, brochures, first contacts, and so on. In this chapter we go further by analysing that most important first impression of all, *the welcome*, and to a lesser extent, *the goodbye*. Both, if achieved successfully, will contribute positively to the other subject of this chapter – what we are actually selling.

Customer care is an essential element of the 'people business'. 'People' means human contact, and this means some form of relationship, speech, body language or facial expression communicated between two people who probably don't know each other but have, for a period of time, to have some kind of discourse together. This all adds up to care that is *active*.

As we have seen, first impressions of a building, a reception desk or even just a car park are made in a few seconds (see Figure 3.1). So, too, are the impressions we make on each other as people. The task of those welcoming customers is that of making them feel genuinely wanted – a friend offering help in need – as soon as possible.

It is no easy task. First, there are the customers themselves. Spend time observing in any reception area, whether it be a garage, doctors or hotel, and you see many uneasy, shy, uncertain people. When a person feels this way, they can easily become unfriendly, reveal a quick temper or be rude if they are not approached or welcomed in the right way.

Second, there is the procedure. So often, this, in itself, can be very unwelcoming. Using a standard form of words in welcome, either on a telephone or face-to-face, can produce automation and, ultimately, boredom for both the incoming customer and the staff. Yes, this may be the ninety-first person you have received or checked in on this shift, but this person should feel as welcome as the first. To this end, it is probably prudent to dispense with the standard words of welcome or departure, instead allowing the staff to use their own (within reason of course). In this way, a far more genuine climate is achieved.

Figure 3.1 Making a positive first impression

The other problem with procedure is often the actual form filling required and the process of getting the new arrival to the office, surgery or bedroom. Of course, today security is extremely important, but it does no harm to check occasionally how the procedures are working. Do the name badges serve their purpose, and, most important, how long does the whole process take?

Third, is the subconscious. No book on customer care is complete without some mention of body language! Sufficient to say here that customers' and staff's facial smiles may be hiding a very different inner feeling. A feeling, perhaps, of mistrust, physical abhorrence, discrimination or simple dislike is visible through our subconscious actions. The step backwards, the shift of the eyes, movements of the hands or arms or a turning away all tell a story to the other party. Somehow, this instinct has to be buried by those welcoming customers. Many achieve this by 'overacting' or relying on automatic phrases and false smiles, but the *best* way to solve the problem is to ensure that the welcomer really *enjoys* the job and working with the people on their team. In this way, many (but not all) the unseen signs on either side are removed.

Finally, there are the words. Many retailers have spent time and money deciding on whether shop assistants should say 'May I help you?', 'How may I help you?' or simply 'What can I get you?' Essentially, the first words to an incoming customer are: 'Good _____. Welcome to _____', followed by a request for the name of the product or service the customer wants. It is *not* a 'Yes?' or 'Next', and neither is it a grunt of recognition!

It is essential also to use 'open questions' – those beginning with 'who', 'what', 'why', 'when', 'which' and 'how'. In this way, the customer *has* to offer a reply other than simply 'Yes' or 'No'. A graphic illustration of this comes from the story of the InterCity trainee Welcome Host gaining early work experience. To travellers at Bristol Temple Meads, his question 'Can I help you?' received only 'No's, grunts or a rapid walking away; but when he asked 'Where are you travelling to?' it resulted in many happy people being helped or escorted to the right train or platform, and probably resulted in them having a very different view of British Rail's efficiency.

Open questions will produce information – the name of the person, their reason for being there, and other useful or meaningful pieces of data that the welcomer can use to make the newcomer relaxed, at ease, and, hopefully, friendly.

For example, the fact that Mr Jones has travelled by car from Wiltshire to London through thick fog on the M4 and is only five minutes late for an important appointment produces three pieces of useful 'welcoming' chat. First, his name, which can now be remembered and used again, second, the opportunity to congratulate him on his fortitude in making the journey, and, third, the chance to reassure him that being just five minutes late doesn't matter. That the welcomer's sister also lives in Swindon and does he know the 'Dog and Duck' at Stratton would *not* be part of good welcoming patter!

It is at this point that the unexpected can make all the difference. One example in the case of Mr Jones would be to offer free use of the phone to tell his partner that he has arrived safely!

The use of names in the welcome can sometimes be a problem. Certainly they have to be used, which is why so much money is spent on badges giving names and titles, but be careful not to overuse them. Using 'Mr Jones' as a welcome and to announce his arrival, is sufficient, but it should not appear in every sentence. It can also be used when he leaves. Whenever it is used it is essential to get it right – all of it! Mr Frederick Jones must not become Cedric Jones!

HELPING THE WELCOME

Providing a well-sited reception desk with a telephone and some 'Visitor' labels is not the end of the story, because, very soon, the system will fail due to lack of information, causing embarrassment to the welcomer and annoyance to the customer.

In today's world of technology, databases, and rapid communication systems, it has to be possible to provide a large amount of information to reception about incoming arrivals (and departures). Most hotels now hold databases on former guests, so that by the time of a second or third visit, the guest is given the same room, certainly their key without asking for it, and, perhaps, their favourite drink, even served by the waiter who chatted to them last time!

To an extent, this can be applied in other types of business. Sending reception details of those coming to a meeting or interview, parcels expected from a printer, even information about someone who has said they will be late so that they can be reassured on arrival creates that extra feeling of care. One company has a board at reception on which is written, _____ Limited today welcomes _____'. It creates an immense feeling of pride within a visitor to see their name written up, but, equally, one of considerable disappointment and annoyance if it's been forgotten!

One important point about the reception desk is to remember that although extra staff can always be a problem in terms of adding to the wages bill, it is wise to check exactly how much work a welcomer has to do – it is not easy to ensure a friendly and efficient welcome for everyone if there are also 700 envelopes to seal or the petty cash statements to type before midday. Nor is it easy if the receptionist is expected to cope with a 150-extension switchboard *and* greet 200 guests a day. Generally, the procedures and the administration take priority over the personal welcomes, so take time to watch how reception actually manages this workload, then decide how much additional work can be undertaken, if any, at the vital front desk.

All these points, however small, create, through welcoming and care, the right climate for *selling*. If the customer experiences feelings of well-being and comfort, they are more than likely to come back again, to do more business, This is a direct result of the welcome and care that was provided on their last visit.

CBI surveys incorporated into English Tourist Board (ETB) Welcome Host programmes have established that as many as 68 per cent of customers stop dealing with firms because the salespeople (the carers) are indifferent and show little interest in them or their problems!

However, we don't just go to a particular hotel or shop because the receptionist has a nice smile! If we were to go to a specialist hi-fi shop, we would expect to receive helpful advice on the merits of various makes of CD player or tape deck. So, selling within the frame of customer care includes such attributes in the carer as:

- expertise
- quick responses
- a helpful, positive attitude
- being confident in their dealings
- a welcoming smile
- being reliable
- having an understanding of the customer's needs
- giving good service
- efficiency
- exhibiting sympathy.

In other words, this calls for a *professional*, taking pride in the job, and pleasure in providing the service and care cheerfully. It is not achieved by the hard sell or the pushy salesperson, but, rather by the subliminal message that says, 'by caring we know that you will come back again to receive the same service'. In this way, greater product sales can be achieved in an increasingly competitive market-place.

The key word is *satisfaction* – for both staff (the server) and customer (the served). The selling with customer care can be summed up, appropriately in the mnemonic PERFECT:

P`= professional
E = efficient
R = reliable
F = friendly
E = expert
C = caring
T = trustworthy.

Finally, some words on the farewell. As was the case with first and last *passive* impressions, the personal contacts at the farewell stage are also vitally important. Again, the procedures, the body language, the words used, and the customers themselves have important parts to play in its success or otherwise. Our words of thanks, a smile or a handshake can say a happy farewell, while our other subconscious actions are saying the opposite – 'The sooner you go (or I get out of here) the better!'

The farewell stage, though, has to leave the right impression, whoever the caller or customer was. A genuine feeling of either sorrow at their departure, pleasure at doing business with them or wishing them luck on their journey is essential. Also, some unexpected action – a small present, keepsake, give-away or whatever – does wonders!

Two things *have* to be said : 'Goodbye' and 'Thank you'. 'Thank you's need to be said however small the deed, to someone delivering the post or a parcel to a major shareholder – all deserve thanks for being there. Remember, too, that the process of expectation begins again as soon as a person leaves one experience. There is a 'looking forward to' feeling about the next time. The more this process can be boosted in your favour, the better are your chances of selling through care in the future. It all goes towards raising the customer's expectations of receiving continued care and service. Remember:

'When my treatment is less than my expectations – that is bad service'
'When my treatment is more than my expectations – that is good service.'

Training activities

· ·

1 MANAGEMENT

Carry out a full review of all the welcome/arrival and farewell/departure procedures. Report on:

● information held on customers/guests

● how it is used in welcoming them

● what happens when they leave – whether or not it is updated

● whether or not all staff expecting visitors notify reception.

● whether or not reception staff have all the necessary information without having to do embarrassing checks

● whether or not reception staff have too much to do

● whether or not the procedures are too cumbersome – check if they interfere in the actual face-to-face contacts

● what 'extras' can be provided to give that 'unexpected' surprise at welcome or departure points.

Figure 3.2 gives an example of the kind of sheet that can be used for such a review.

Ask your management team to decide for themselves what the company is actually selling and discuss the results in relation to the PERFECT mnemonic.

2 STAFF

The welcome exercise

To get everyone thinking in the same way start with this exercise. Hand out a piece of paper to each trainee. Get them to write the letters W, E, L, C, O, M, and E down the left-hand side of the paper. Now give them five minutes or so to think of as many words or phrases beginning with each of these letters that mean 'welcome' to them as they can. On completion, list all the words on a flip chart. It is surprising how many there are. Here are some examples.

Figure 3.2 Example of management review sheet to use to assess care given during arrival/departure of customers/guests

Activity	How handled/ appearance 1–10 marks	Remarks	Second check 1–10 marks (must improve rating)
1 Outside signage			
2 General appearance			
3 Car park area			
4 Other visible road areas			
5 Receiving bay			
6 Doorways			
7 Passageways			
8 Internal signage			
9 Toilets/wash areas			
10 Physical welcome			
11 Handling skills			
12 Length of waiting time			
13 Departure/leaving procedure			
14 Paperwork complete/ in order			

Note

By looking at these areas and completing the check-list, a thorough review of the welcome/departure procedure, and how customers are cared for, can be achieved. Decide the number of marks to award on a scale of 1–10 and what mark constitutes a failure (below 4, say). A second check, a month later, should produce an improvement of at least 50 per cent.

W = welcome, willing, worthy, witty (but not too much), waiting, watching, warm, well-meaning, wavelength

E = eye contact, enthusiasm, engaging, effusive, ease

L = lively, looking at/up, liking, lasting

C = cheerful, cordial, careful, chatty (but not too much!), civil, clear, clean, complimentary, celebrate, congenial

O = obliging, observant, open, on friendly terms, open door, outgoing

M = merry, memorable, make friends, mean well, matter, meet, mix, make time, manner

E = efficient, entertaining, effort, expressive.

If the first *physical* impression can create problems for a customer, the first *personal* contact can *really* be troublesome.

Ask your trainees to recount any good or bad welcoming experiences and make notes of the essential points, like smiles, words of welcome, expressions, how they dealt with them.

Now begin to build up a 'code of practice' for the welcome process in the company, which can include the following.

1 *Read the signs* How does the customer seem as they approach you? You only have a short time to get the first words right. Does the person look lost, happy/annoyed, do you know them?
2 *Greet* Good morning/afternoon. If you know the customer's name, use it; if not, find out quickly then use it (but don't overdo it). Smile and be friendly.
3 *Find out* Discover the purpose of the visit, then quickly deal with any procedures, such as signing in, name badges, registration or whatever if they are in reception. Try not to let any necessary security procedures interfere with the welcome procedure. If you are dealing personally with the customer, go straight on to sort out the needs, for example, complete the purchase, advise on availability, and so on.
4 *Advise* Tell the customer what is happening, for example, if they have to be kept waiting, perhaps offer refreshment.
5 *Deal* Finish the encounter with what has to be done – show the person to an office or whatever – meeting the identified need as efficiently as possible.

Remember to maintain your interest in the customer at all times and to be a friendly face. Most customers are unsure of themselves, they are in a strange place, and need help. A useful way to remember the welcome process is to use another mnemonic:

SAPID = Smile, Acknowledge, find Purpose, keep Interested and Deal with the need

See Figure 3.3 for an example of a check-list to use to improve the welcome and departure. Memorizing such a list is very helpful.

Figure 3.3 A personal welcome/departure check-list

> **The welcome/departure given to customers**
>
> **Do I . . .**
>
> know who is coming to the company today, are they regulars, important, who are they visiting?
>
> know their names and use them once known?
>
> have a list with times of arrival (putting names on a board to make them feel extra welcome)?
>
> check all the area – toilets, and so on – to ensure a good welcome?
>
> check all areas for health, safety, and security?
>
> wear my uniform/smart clothes in order to represent the company efficiently?
>
> provide a genuine welcome to all comers by giving them a warm smile?
>
> know the incoming procedure – register, visitors' book, badges, and so on?
>
> quickly advise relevant people of arrivals?
>
> maintain a regular check on my area?
>
> not become swamped with extra work to the detriment of visitors' needs?
>
> provide additional support to visitors if they are kept waiting?
>
> know all the emergency/security procedures and what to do if suspicions are aroused?
>
> thank those leaving and wish them well?
>
> know departure procedures – badge collection, other paperwork, and so on?
>
> know location of taxis and other transport providers?
>
> know any local road/rail problems to advise visitors about on departure?
>
> take a pride in my job as the first and last contact with _____ Company?

Role plays

To bring home the welcome process, use two or more of the following role plays. After each, ask the trainees who did not take part in the role play to comment on the way the welcome was undertaken. Ask the 'customer' how they felt they were treated and the 'staff' how they thought they had been handled.

☞ *Role play 1*

Customer

You are a businessman coming to a seaside town for a conference. Your accommodation has been booked for you in an hotel you don't know. Your journey down has been a nightmare – there has been heavy rain and wind, several delays due to accidents, and you had a bad experience in a motorway service station. You eventually find your way to the hotel, but bad signing and lighting mean that you miss the entrance to the car park and have to go round the block again. On parking, you step right into a puddle. As you come into the hotel, the receptionist has her back to you and is on the phone. Some welcome you think!

Figure 3.4 Is it the equipment or the receptionist who is creating the bad impression for the incoming guest?

Staff

Since coming on duty three hours ago, things have been very difficult for you as a receptionist at a busy seaside hotel. There is a big conference tomorrow, but many of the guests have been delayed by the bad weather. The phone has hardly stopped (when you answer it you have to turn away from the desk). You are dealing with a call when you become aware that there is someone at the desk.

Talking points

What about the phone? Is this another example of equipment upsetting first impressions? (see Figure 3.4)

How did the receptionist cope? Did they show how difficult the shift had been? How was the customer handled? Was the customer satisfied?

☞ Role play 2

Staff

You are an assistant in a travel enquiry office. You are approached by a rather lost and foreign tourist with a guide book and phrase book (you can only speak English)!

Customer

You are a foreign tourist on your first visit to this country, and you have little knowledge of the language. You are desperate to change some currency and the person in the enquiry office looks friendly, perhaps they can help.

Talking points

The difficulties of foreign languages! How do we cope? How does the welcome fare under *these* circumstances?

☞ Role play 3

Staff

You are the Receptionist/Telephonist in a busy company's entrance foyer. In addition to receiving many incoming calls, you have to undertake extra typing and addressing of envelopes at the moment because of staff shortages.

Today has been frantic, and now you just have to frank and post all the mail before 5.00 pm. You are suddenly aware that someone is standing at your desk.

Customer

You have been stuck in traffic and, as a result, arrive nearly half an hour late for an important 4.30 pm appointment. The car park, which is dirty and full of litter, is full so you are in a bad temper and flustered when you get to the reception desk. The Receptionist is more interested in answering the phone and franking the mail than in seeing you. After several moments, you can wait no longer and cough loudly.

Talking points

Perhaps this is a typical example of the 'welcome' receptionist having too much to do and so not remembering that the visitor due at 4.30 hadn't arrived (even if they had been told!) The message is that, maybe, more staff or other staff are needed to sort out the post.

☞ Role play 4a

Staff

You are just about to go off duty from the early reception shift in a busy hotel. The telephone rings and it is a bad line. What sounds like a Mr Timms is telling you that he will not be arriving until much later because he has to go to an extra meeting. You take the call and leave a quick note for your relief, a new member of staff (who is next door, having a cup of tea).

Customer

Your name is Mr Symms and you are a regular visitor to this hotel. An extra meeting has been called today, which means you will be very late arriving at the hotel. You ring from your car phone (the line is bad) and you advise the hotel accordingly.

Talking point

A straightforward telephone call, which should be correctly handled.

☞ *Role play 4b*

Customer

Again, you are Mr Symms and you have now arrived, very late, at the hotel, where you are a regular guest. A new receptionist, who you have not seen before, is just balancing the books, and when you request your room you are told that it has been released and the hotel is now full.

Staff

You are a new receptionist at this hotel. This evening has been very busy and, as a result, all the rooms have been booked and sold, including all those reserved by non-arrivals after 7.00 pm. The early shift left a note about a Mr Timms, but as no one of that name is booked, you assume it is an old note and destroy it. It is now 11.00 pm, you are finally balancing prior to going to bed when a man called Mr Symms arrives demanding his room, claiming he rang earlier to say he would be late.

Talking points

The lack of communication, slackness at the end of a shift, especially as the relief is a new, inexperienced member of staff. Never trust a bad telephone line. Let's hope there is one emergency room left!

☞ *Role play 5*

Customer

It is a busy morning at the Porter's Desk. You queue up to collect a paper and leave your room key before going to your first appointment. The Porter has been trained by rote and repeats the same message to each person. You collect your paper and are so mesmerized by the performance that you forget to give in your key. So, you go back in, discover that the Porter doesn't recognize you and gives you the same message . You decide to discuss things with him!

Staff

You are the new Porter in a hotel and your Boss had told you to say the same messages to everyone each morning. These are 'Good morning, how may I help you? My name is Paul, which paper do you require?', then 'Thank you, have a nice day!' Today some 30 people have seen you, when a man, who looks vaguely familiar decides to challenge you.

Talking points

Real training does not involve saying things learned by rote; a person's personality and natural talent will not become apparent unless they are allowed to be genuine.

☞ Role play 6

Staff

You have come to work today in a very bad mood. You have had a row with your partner, your bus was late, there is heavy rain, you have the beginnings of a cold and your supervisor has had a go at you about your appearance. Now this stupid visitor is having another go at you because you ignored him and he claims you are very rude. You must defend yourself.

Customer

You arrive at this company to have an important meeting with the Managing Director. The Receptionist is looking very sullen, somewhat untidy, and doesn't appear to be in the best of tempers. They also slam down the phone to someone and ignore you for several minutes before looking up and saying, 'Yes?'

Talking points

Full attention must be given to the work – leave the moods behind. When is the best time to discipline staff? Did the Receptionist know how important this visitor was?

Last impressions

To complete this section of training, we now need to look at the *ends* of all the exchanges and the procedures, and at how our customers feel when they leave us.

We have welcomed them, looked at and after them, found out what they wanted and provided it for them. The customers *should* be satisfied, but *are* they? How do we find out?

Answer: ask them! Easy, but do we?

A lot of people will not come back or will not recommend us to others simply because they were not properly 'greeted' on their departure. Ask the trainees what percentage of customers don't come back because of bad service (see page 119). So:

- we need to make sure that every customer, however short or long their time with us, is spoken to before they leave
- we need to find out whether or not they were satisfied with the service – did they get what they wanted, see the person necessary or whatever.
- above all, they need to hear two important things: 'Goodbye' and 'Thank you'.

Again, ask your trainees what their last impressions of a customer experience have been. Normally the final impression helps a customer to remember (hopefully) the good points and prompts a desire to return.

The last impression needs to be *satisfaction*, a feeling of well-being, of being looked after, and sent on their way feeling as if someone actually cares, that they matter to you. This has to be communicated in the last few exchanges, before a customer leaves – again, this is assisted by the physical things outside, like clear exit signs, ease of leaving the car park, directions to the railway station, personal giveaways, perhaps, even a packed lunch for a long journey!

The process of expectation begins again at departure, and if the care and attention has been good, the customer is likely to return.

Finally, examine with your trainees how departing customers are handled and ask them to suggest any changes or improvements.

Case study

Use this as a means to draw together all the training points raised in this chapter.

THE NOT SO 'LIVE WIRE' RETAILER

J. J. Scroggs is a small but specialist electrical retailer still holding its own against the larger chains, mainly because of its regular customers and a reputation for past achievements of its six branches.

Recession has bitten hard, aided by a major chain opening large superstores out of town. Many staff have left and there is now a much younger staff complement, several part-timers, and inexperienced managers.

The stores open late every Tuesday for training purposes, but many now use this as an excuse to arrive late.

As Area Manager for three of the stores, you are beginning to receive many complaints regarding lack of expertise, customers having to wait a long time, requests for refunds because the wrong product has been delivered, and now the financial results, which have shown some resilience until now, are beginning to show serious losses.

You decide to make a surprise visit to two of the stores. You discover few staff know you, or you them, the level of service skill is poor, and many customers browse then leave without purchasing anything. Something *has* to be done, urgently.

Your task

As Area Manager, draw up a plan to right the problems and say how you would sell your ideas to the managers you control. In particular, how are you or they to encourage more customers, what skills will the staff need, and how can you stimulate more action in the Tuesday training sessions. What timescale will you set and how will you prioritize the action to be taken.

Look again at the attributes needed to sell through care, thus encouraging repeat custom, and so on. Also, consider how product expertise and staff motivation can be encouraged. How can the company become *perfect* and sell *satisfaction*.

4

QUALITY AND STANDARDS OF CARE

INTRODUCTION

So far in this book we have, in a nutshell, established that standards of care have to apply throughout an organization and affect every aspect of the staff's, manager's and customer's contacts. They have to apply from the top to the bottom of an organization and be capable of being measured, monitored, and reviewed.

All are essential ingredients of an effective, quality operation. We have also seen that certain skills are necessary to sell to customers within a framework of care as they will have gone through various processes, either consciously or subconsciously, before they are at the point of being welcomed by the estab-

Figure 4.1 It is important to set standards of care

lishment. To assist in meeting their needs, particularly at the crucial welcome and departure stages – a sense of *belonging* and *belief* in the company is needed by every member of the service staff. This can be achieved by providing good care of customers by staff from the first day of employment.

To some, providing an effective welcome and continuous care is a matter of plain common sense and natural ability. To others this may be hard work, with plenty of opportunities to argue with, or upset, customers who 'dare' not play the right game! If left unchecked, therefore, such differences in care of customers by staff can lead to a hopeless mess of uncertainty and, ultimately, poor standards and many complaints.

So, customer care is very much part of the 1990s, of defined quality and standards. Setting such standards and maintaining quality are therefore issues that are essential to this book.

WHAT IS QUALITY CARE?

To answer this question, four dictionary definitions of the word 'quality' are worth considering:

- *a skill or faculty* how good we are at doing things, what quality of skills are possessed by the carers
- *social standing or rank* what position the company holds in the care league
- *distinctive character* what reputation the company has and how different it is from the competition
- *degree of excellence* how close the degree of care is to the ultimate – excellence.

In striving to provide the best-quality care, therefore, skilled staff are needed in order to give a company a reputation and standing in the ratings, providing the right sort of service and care to the customer.

The problem is that providing service and care to *people* means that you have to take account of personal preferences on both sides – recognize that piece of human chemistry which makes two people actually relate positively to each other. In most service environments, we are either handling, receiving or adding value to a manufactured product or providing the material or the product ourselves and then serving the customer as well. Checks are almost invariably made on the quality of products either made or received, but it is still relatively unusual to carry out checks on the service given.

A good example of a typical service problem was highlighted in *The Times'* Saturday Magazine (January 1994) by Lynne Truss, one of its feature writers:

Can we have the table in the window please?

On Wednesday, I meet a friend for lunch in a smart restaurant, and although the place is virtually empty, we find we are guided firmly to a table at the back. The sense of annoyance is familiar. Big, loud, professional women dining without men are nearly always offered discreet little tables next to the cutlery or convenient for the gents. It's a sort-of unwritten rule.

Anyway, our sullen waitress does not respond. Recklessly, we repeat our request. 'That table in the window, is it free?'

She purses her lips. She looks at us, looks at the window, looks back at us again, and emits a sigh.

'Well, all right,' she concedes sulkily. 'But really it's reserved in case somebody else turns up.'

We exchange glances. This is not an auspicious beginning, and, alas, things do not improve thereafter; we have hardly settled in front of our menus before we discover that, yet again, we have failed to be the right people in the right place.

'The soup and the trout are off,' she says. 'Well, they're not off exactly; I mean we haven't run out. It's just that we're reserving them in case some other people want to eat them later.' Our jaws drop, but she doesn't notice. When she has gone, we briefly consider how to proceed. 'Pay for our lunch? Don't think so. After all, it would hardly be fair on the other people to deprive them of the option.'

Later, having dined miserably from the tiny choice left available on the menu, we notice that some people at the next table are eating artichokes. We ask the waitress why we weren't offered them.

'Oh, that's from the à la carte,' she explains offhandedly. 'Which we don't give out'.

So, in our quest for the answer to our question about what quality care is, we now have two sides of the triangle (Figure 4.2) : the *product* (the raw material or purchased goods coming into or produced within a unit to a given quality level, checked against a specification) and the *service* (provided to add value to this product).

Figure 4.2 Two sides of the triangle of quality care

Figure 4.3 The third side of the triangle – the customers

The third element, of course, is the customers (Figure 4.3), who are attracted to buy the product because of its reputation and quality, and by the service provided.

Surrounding the triangle of these three elements is the control function – essential in all matters of quality – provided by management to check the quality continually (Figure 4.4).

So, quality care can be defined, first, as, 'Providing products and services that satisfy customer needs'. But for how long? Products and services are not static and customers' needs change. Therefore, a better definition may be, 'Satisfying customer expectations by continually improving products and service'. Certainly better, but at what cost? Thus, a third definition of quality care is, 'Continually meeting agreed customer requirements for products and service within best cost limits'.

The mention of *costs* focuses our attention on the very crucial topic of *customers*, as we cannot provide customer service without limiting costs in some way, so three important questions need to be asked – and answered, of course – as accurately as possible.

- Who are the *customers*?
- Why do they come to us?
- What do they want?

Figure 4.4 The control function ensures that a high quality of care is maintained

So often, the message from service companies is one of 'Don't worry, it's only a customer' – a nuisance, another drain on our bottom line! Instead, the message should be one of trying to identify, carefully, the present and future customers our service or product attracts. Subsequently, it should also be to find out, clearly, what they expect from us and then search out and provide a service that matches these expectations, focusing the *care* element exactly where it is wanted, and ensuring that costs or budgets are not exceeded.

Having answered these questions as accurately as possible – and it isn't easy – it becomes important to pinpoint the resources available or that will be needed to meet the expectations that have been identified. Very often, the opposite has been the case, that is care staff or a care policy have been applied where the company *thinks* these are most needed. This wastes resources and does not meet the real needs and expectations of customers. A simple example of this is providing wonderfully trained, welcoming staff at a reception desk, but poorly trained staff to operate the switchboard when most enquiries come through on the telephone. Another is providing an excellent customer service centre at a bus or railway station, but not giving up-to-date information or care training to those inspectors or platform staff seeing customers on to the buses or trains.

So, if we have defined who our customers are and what their expectations are, how do we decide how to use and deploy our resources so that we can 'continually meet agreed customer requirements for products and service within best cost limits'?

Answer, involve all the individuals and all the activities in planning where and how they will best meet customers' needs and expectations. In other words, set up an internal support system to ensure that customer care is focused where it is most needed, and, just as important, those involved in providing it are committed to care and believe in it (remember the CICC system of Chapter 1).

One way in which everyone can be involved in this planning is to extend the training activities given in Chapter 1. In this chapter we shall explore actually setting and monitoring standards of care, which are essential if care is to be properly controlled (see Training and operational activities, later in this chapter).

Total quality care is made up of a number (quantity) of care standards. These can be agreed and written down so that they are clearly understood by everyone (particularly if they have been involved in setting them).

It is important to stress that there are two levels:

- a minimum, which produces a *reasonable* degree of satisfaction
- a degree of excellence towards which everyone should strive.

Between the two there has to be some element of flexibility, so that the carer can meet the particular needs of a customer at that precise moment, never falling below the minimum standards laid down and within the 'best cost limits', but, perhaps, not going for out and out excellence.

This practice is now gaining ground in the guise of 'empowerment', which is allowing managers and staff 'to think for themselves' when trying to satisfy customer needs. The breakfast waitress who reduces the customer's bill because there was a delay, the receptionist using their own car to take a guest to an airport, the electrician putting that little bit extra effort into making a repair to enhance the quality of service, all without recourse to authority, are operating in this way, making instant decisions with confidence because they know the company's parameters regarding care of customers.

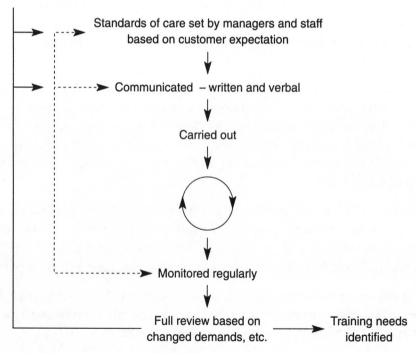

Figure 4.5 The cycle of control for care of customers

CARE STANDARDS

There are some essential guidelines for setting standards. They must be:

- *realistic* you cannot achieve the impossible
- *descriptive* explain what can and should be achieved
- *understood* clear, concise, with proper guidance
- *properly communicated* in an easy to understand form, written down, and circulated to everyone
- *capable of measurement* by all those involved, including the customer.

Moreover there must be a regular system of monitoring and review to reflect changes in care demands, staff ability or new product ranges.

The ultimate responsibility for monitoring and review must be that of management, but staff – and, indeed, customers – have a role to play in ensuring that the quality and standards of care are focused in the right place. The 'cycle of control' (see Figure 4.5) illustrates how this is achieved.

Care surveys

Customers can play a large part in monitoring the quality and standards of care. The problem is getting and keeping their interest and making it worth their while. A long and complicated questionnaire will probably only attract the professional complainer who has an axe to grind and a desire for publicity and attention.

A short, easily completed form with some opportunity of a prize (free drink, discount, tokens towards something more meaningful) is likely to attract a wider audience. The ultimate, of course, is for the care to be so good that customers feel the need to comment on it.

Whatever the response, it is very important to:

- take careful note of all replies
- contact each respondent and thank them for their trouble, putting right any shortcomings to their satisfaction
- analyse the good and bad points
- circulate the results to all concerned, however trivial the comments
- ensure that action is taken to correct or amend gaps in care
- make it as easy as possible for the customer to respond.

It is important to take the results of customer feedback very seriously. Analysis of it will identify weak areas, even the weak member of staff on duty at the time. Many companies go to great trouble to analyse such questionnaires, noting the number circling each grade on the questionnaire scale, the percentage commenting on the performance of each department, the improvement, decrease from previous months, and so on (for an example of a brief questionnaire, see Figure 4.6).

Figure 4.6 Example of a customer questionnaire

Thank you for using our _____ .

In order that we can continue to provide you with the best possible service in the future, I would be very grateful if you could spend a short time completing the questions below. All replies will be entered in our prize draw for _____ .

Please tick the relevant box.

	Excellent	Good	Reasonable	Poor
1 Quality of welcome. Any comments.	☐	☐	☐	☐
2 Initial contact with staff. Additional comments.	☐	☐	☐	☐
3 Order taking. Additional comments.	☐	☐	☐	☐
4 Knowledge of product. Additional comments.	☐	☐	☐	☐
5 Standard of service. Additional comments.	☐	☐	☐	☐
6 Completion of transaction. Additional comments.	☐	☐	☐	☐
7 Overall comments.	☐	☐	☐	☐

Thank you very much for your help. Please place the completed form in the box provided, or send to FREEPOST XYZ.

It is also vital to ensure that *everyone* gets a copy of the analysis, discusses it at staff or management meetings and feeds back any comments or improvements that result. Those responsible for instituting quality and standards of care should also take note of all complaint and compliment letters or comments. So often, it is only the complaints that filter down, but both kinds of feedback from customers are of equal importance and should be displayed on noticeboards for all to see (Figure 4.7).

Recruitment to care positions

One essential message of this chapter is that we need to identify our customers' present or future, actual or potential needs, wants or desires, and convert this knowledge into action by making the right decisions about resources and how we organize ourselves to meet these desired levels of care.

The key resource for achieving this is, of course, *staff*, yet many companies do not take account of what customers expect or want when they select staff to provide this service.

Figure 4.7 Comments from customers – complaints *and* compliments – should be made available to all staff having contact with customers

The assistant in the electrical shop who has no idea how a washing machine works, the telephonist with a short temper, the receptionist with an abrupt manner, all have their many equals in today's service industries. Much can be overcome by good training, but how much better it is to clearly define what personal characteristics staff need to possess if they are to be effective in positions involving the care of customers.

Obviously, the laws relating to discrimination and fair recruitment policies must be followed, but, providing the company knows the sorts of customers, their expectations, and demands, it is possible, using the well-tried 'personnel specification' system, to lay down minimum and ideal requirements when recruiting staff to meet these needs.

The seven main points to bear in mind are:

- *physical* bearing, stature, physical stamina
- *attainments* education and training
- *general intelligence* ability to be creative, think things through, use judgement
- *special attributes* technical skills or knowledge, acquired from other jobs, and so on.
- *interests* leisure or outside activities, team involvement
- *disposition* expectations, stability, achievements
- *circumstances* special work experience/conditions, domestic, such as amount of travel involved, home commitments, and so on.

Compiling an 'ideal person' specification for the care positions linked to customer care needs will highlight three basic measures relating to each job so examined:

- the *essential* elements of a person's ability or background, those indispensable to a job
- the *desirable* elements – less essential, but useful to have
- the *'contraindications'* – things that will disqualify an applicant from the job.

The ideal person specification will also highlight what the content of a job advertisement should be and assist the early sorting of the applications of the respondents.

At the interview stage, following further weeding out and pruning, those on the short list can be given various exercises, role plays or case studies to work through that are based on the customer needs, in order to identify how suitable, or otherwise, they are for the positions.

This process is obviously expensive and time-consuming, but if this is set against the inconvenience, publicity (and cost and time) of investigating complaints, dealing with irate customers and re-recruiting, it soon becomes clear that it is well worth it. Moreover, if staff have been correctly recruited, it is usual for them to stay in the job and develop new and better skills because the work and the person suit each other.

In conclusion, six principles are essential if quality care is to be given to customers:

1 customers' present and future (actual and potential) requirements need to be identified
2 customer expectations need to be clearly defined
3 stemming from the above, it is necessary to be able to identify and provide a service that matches these needs and expectations
4 decisions taken regarding resources and organization need to be based on the perceived expectations (not the other way round)
5 everyone and all activities need to be involved in making these decisions
6 a system for achieving success through sound recruitment and clearly agreed and defined standards of quality care, should be developed.

Training and operational activities

∙∙∙

1 MANAGEMENT

Having now arrived at the company's definition of care, the time has come to link this to a definition of what constitutes *quality* care.

Using the four dictionary definitions (see page 66), divide your team up into small groups and ask them to say how good the company is at doing things – what position the company holds in the care league, what its reputation is, and how close to or far from 'excellent' is the quality of care we give.

Once decided, discuss the results and use them to produce an agreed definition of quality care for the whole company, then how it is to be communicated to everyone and how it should be monitored.

Detail each manager responsible for the products produced or served and the service provided to review their activities. How good are the raw materials or those products made from them? Is the quality right – does it meet the new definition?

What about the service – where are the gaps, does it actually add value, does everyone involved play their part? Receive reports back and decide what action has to be taken.

Customers

(Supplement to the training activities of Chapter 1.)

Ask your managers (again in small groups) to answer the questions posed on page 68.

For the question 'Who are the customers?', the replies may produce a variety of responses, (for, say, regulars get them to say how many, age range or group, types – leisure, business, passing trade, such as tourists, or specialist users).

For 'Why do they come to us?', consider things like service, friendliness, price, discounts, facilities, availability, location, attitude of staff, reputation, delivery record, hours of opening, and so on.

For 'What do they want?', the answers are likely to be, primarily, quality, care, speed of response, efficiency, information, standards, and so on.

Once the questions have been answered, look at the gaps – what customers are we missing and why, what other service could we provide and how, and how can other groups be persuaded to come to us?

Setting standards of care

Set up small working groups of staff and managers with the brief of setting care standards throughout the organization. They should be challenging but achievable. Make sure there is a strict timetable for completion and that the group includes how the standards are to be:

● trained in and communicated

● made operational

● monitored and reviewed

● kept up to date.

Figure 4.8 Example of a list of care standards

Care task/activity	Minimum standard to be achieved	When/how checked
Answering telephone	Three rings, maximum, before answered	'Mystery caller' regularly
Answering incoming letters	First reply given within two days	Manager to check post book
Welcoming at reception	Acknowledged within 30 seconds	Manager to check
Ensuring toilets clean and 'welcoming'	Cleaned/checked every hour with signed declaration	Supervisor to inspect
Ensuring staff have key skills and knowledge of products	Full awareness of care standards. Able to deal fully with at least three major products	Regular quiz to test knowledge

The pro forma of Figure 4.8 is just one small example of how agreed care standards can be set out. You can add as many other columns as necessary, for example as a training check.

It is vitally important that, once agreed, all staff and managers have copies of the standards and know what they have to achieve (like the member of staff in Figure 4.9).

Customer questionnaires

If you have them, review their use, or misuse, then have your team redesign the questions. Look at what happens to them, how they are communicated, what notice is taken of them, what follow-ups and action occur, and so on.

If you do *not* have questionnaires, decide whether one or more would be worth while and how to use them. Commission a group to design one and test it over a period, monitoring the results. Consult everyone about what to include.

Figure 4.9 Staff need to absorb standards of care that have been decided in order to give quality care to customers

Personnel specifications

Look at every job within the company that involves care.

Look at the answers given to the 'Who are the customers?' question earlier. Ask 'Do we employ the right staff to meet the needs of who we perceive to be our customers?'

Produce seven-point personnel specifications for each job title and devise new interview procedures, application forms, and advertisements to achieve the ideal match.

Decide how any staff who do *not* match up to the specifications can be trained to meet the new standards.

There now follow some examples of personnel specifications for care jobs. Following these are examples of how these subsequently influenced the wording of job advertisements for these positions.

Hotel receptionist

- *Physical* Of neat appearance, showing some care regarding colour co-ordination of clothes; upright; perhaps a little extrovert, medium height (to establish eye contact easily with customers when standing), fit and keen to remain so to meet needs of job, adaptable when faced with change.
- *Attainments* Preferably able to show ability in English, maths, and a foreign language; six months' experience in a similiar position.
- *General intelligence* Able to demonstrate an ability to think clearly, and cope in a crisis (probe for any examples of this); evidence of involvement in useful hobbies, pastimes; willing to take psychometric test.
- *Special attributes* Preferably to hold City and Guilds Reception Certificate or BTEC Diploma; Knowledge of front-office computer systems; hotel back-ground preferred.
- *Interests* Show interest in leisure activities (to relieve job stress), preferably in team environment.
- *Disposition* Keen to succeed and give long service, eager for promotion or new challenges; no evidence of short time previous jobs.
- *Circumstances* Physically fit to withstand shift patterns; preferably few home problems; lives within five miles of work.

The advertisement for a hotel receptionist

XYZ Hotel seeks applications for a hotel receptionist to join a busy team, working shifts.

Ideally the successful applicant will hold a City and Guilds Reception Certificate and have experience of the .... computer system. Experience in a similiar position is desirable. We pride ourselves on the care we provide for our guests, which is spearheaded by our front desk, so an ability to get on well with people and team members is essential.

Opportunities for promotion are available.

A live out position, the successful applicant will be expected to live within five miles of the Hotel.

Further details about the post are available from ....

Figure 4.10 Example of an advertisement for a position based on the personnel specifications drawn up for that post

Sales assistant for an electrical retailer

- *Physical* Neat in appearance; able to withstand long hours on a shop floor; uniform provided; fit and healthy.

- *Attainments* Some financial expertise, also knowledge of basic electrical standards, safety, and so on, in order to deal with minor customer queries; training given on store products, but basic knowledge of 'white goods' essential.

- *General intelligence* Able to think and converse clearly; civil and polite; cool in a crisis.

- *Special attributes* Preferably hold either/or both an Electrical or Retail NVQ to Level 2 Standard or be willing to take them. Some knowledge of Hoover, Morphy Richards, Electrolux, and Swan products desirable.

- *Interests* Keen on team activities and mixing with/liking of people.

- *Disposition* Preferably able to stay in the job for some time with eventual promotion; some previous evidence of reasonable service length.

- *Circumstances* Live within easy travelling distance of work.

The advertisement for a sales assistant for an electrical retailer

---

The ABC Organization seeks a sales assistant for its Electrical Department.

Previous experience in a similar post desirable, with knowledge of the major 'white goods' products (training will be given on the company's own brands).

The successful candidate will be expected to provide full advice and guidance to customers and, therefore, a good attitude to customer care is essential.

Preference will be given to those already holding an Electrical or Retailing NVQ.

Promotion is possible within the company's training scheme for the right candidate.

Apply in writing to ....

Figure 4.11 Example of an advertisement written along the lines of the personnel specifications for the post

2 STAFF

Carry out the first, third, and fourth exercises/training sessions under management tasks specifications, page 80. Compare the results of these with those of the management group and investigate any discrepancies. (Staff are often nearer to the customers than the managers and so can provide worthwhile insights.)

Figure 4.12 includes a number of personal standards for staff that are necessary if they are to provide the best care for customers. At regular intervals, staff should rate themselves for each, using the scale, then show the results to their Manager or Supervisor who can arrange any necessary 'top-up' training.

Standard-setting exercise

Form groups of three – one to take the management role, one the supervisory role, and one that of the customers. Decide on a regular activity, say, serving coffee at a conference, investigating a complaint, sending out mail-order goods, taking and processing an order.

Figure 4.12 Example of a personal standard of care questionnaire for staff to monitor their performance in this area

---

CUSTOMER CARE QUESTIONNAIRE

Rate your personal standards of care on the scale of 1 to 4:

1 = always
2 = the occasional slip
3 = several mishaps
4 = poor care rating.

Personal standards   *Rating*

1 I always make sure I am neat and tidy.
    □ 1   □ 2   □ 3   □ 4

2 I am always presentable to customers.
    □ 1   □ 2   □ 3   □ 4

3 I always welcome new customers.
    □ 1   □ 2   □ 3   □ 4

4 I enjoy talking to/dealing with regular customers.
    □ 1   □ 2   □ 3   □ 4

5 I am a good member of the team.
    □ 1   □ 2   □ 3   □ 4

6 I am quick and efficient at my work.
    □ 1   □ 2   □ 3   □ 4

7 I know all the products the company sells.
    □ 1   □ 2   □ 3   □ 4

8 I always respond to customer's needs.
    □ 1   □ 2   □ 3   □ 4

9 I know the company care standards.
    □ 1   □ 2   □ 3   □ 4

10 I always enjoy my job.
    □ 1   □ 2   □ 3   □ 4

11 I deal efficiently with difficult customers.
    □ 1   □ 2   □ 3   □ 4

12 I deal efficiently with complaints.
    □ 1   □ 2   □ 3   □ 4

13 I am tactful, patient, and sincere.
    □ 1   □ 2   □ 3   □ 4

14 I always help colleagues in my team.
    □ 1   □ 2   □ 3   □ 4

Figure 4.12 Cont'd

Personal standards		Rating		
15 I know the company procedures.	☐ 1	☐ 2	☐ 3	☐ 4
16 I always look after departing customers.	☐ 1	☐ 2	☐ 3	☐ 4
17 I always carry out the necessary paperwork.	☐ 1	☐ 2	☐ 3	☐ 4
18 I am always confident and caring.	☐ 1	☐ 2	☐ 3	☐ 4
19 I always try to sell through care.	☐ 1	☐ 2	☐ 3	☐ 4
20 I am always good at my job.	☐ 1	☐ 2	☐ 3	☐ 4

Brief the *'management'* to lay down the operational and procedural standards for the task, considering the care needed, numbers of staff, process, and so on.

Brief the *'supervisors'* to think up as many questions as possible for the 'management' to ensure that they are clear on how the job is to be done and the quality expected. Then, 'management' and 'supervisors' publicly negotiate how it is to be achieved and to what standard.

Meanwhile, brief the *'customers'* to consider all that they want in terms of care and quality – not the operational points – speed, politeness, added extras, greeting, getting satisfaction.

In the follow-up, the 'customers' present these needs to the 'management' and 'supervisors'.

The result should be a realization that standards and quality care is not all about operational efficiency. The needs and wants of customers are vital – they will prefer politeness to procedure, thoroughness to speed, an easy smile to first-class dour efficiency.

Get the group to draw conclusions from the exercise and apply the lessons to everyday jobs.

Case study

By participating in the analysis of this case study, staff can see how important the implementation of standards of care is to customer satisfaction.

POOR STANDARDS

The Fortune Roadside Bistro has accepted a booking for a coach party *en route to* the Lake District for a holiday.

There are to be 53 people requiring coffee and biscuits, with only the driver wanting tea. Time is short, so the party will only stay 30 minutes in order to reach their destination in good time.

Some days before the party is due to arrive the organizer, Mr Brewer, rings to order 10 teas (3 fruit teas and 7 ordinary). He also mentions that there will be 2 disabled, elderly passengers who will require a ramp.

On the day, the coach is seriously delayed due to fog and a traffic jam caused by an accident, and so the party eventually arrives an hour late.

Mr Brewer then discovers that no ramp has been provided, and only the 3 fruit teas are available. Several members of the party complain about the state of the toilets, the queue for the telephones, and the lack of seating (this is because another party booked for the same day has arrived on time, but which happens to clash with the time Mr Brewer's party has appeared).

Further trouble erupts when one of the party spills hot coffee over herself and there is no first aider on duty. Several don't receive coffee because of lack of time. In the end Mr Brewer's party leaves, very unhappy.

Three days later, Mr Brewer writes a long letter of complaint and refuses to pay the bill until a satisfactory explanation has been given.

Your task

What's happened? Make some suggestions.

If you were on the Fortune Bistro's staff, how would you reply to Mr Brewer?

Set some standards for coach party breaks involving management, supervisors, staff, and customer requirements.

☞ *Talking points*

Obviously there has been a severe communication breakdown, and this has been compounded by the difficult operational problems caused by the delays to one party.

How many staff were on duty?

When it became apparent that one party was going to be late, this should have meant someone realizing that difficulties could occur and arranging extra seating and so on.

The standards follow the operational requirements of the managers and staff, but look carefully again at what the customers actually want here – speed of service, a sit down, clean toilets, telephones, a drink, and a change of scene!

Set some action plans

Ask each staff member to go away and think about what sort of service they actually provide. Could what they do be done better – are there any gaps, what suggestions can they make to improve things, what help do they need (training or operational changes) to enable them to perform better, and so on? Set a time limit, then discuss the replies to these questions and agree the action to be taken.

5

....

THE SKILLS AND COMPETENCIES REQUIRED FOR CUSTOMER CARE

WHAT STAFF NEED TO GIVE QUALITY CARE

So far in this book we have looked at theories and processes, at common-sense solutions, and the everyday training or operational requirements staff in contact with customers need in order that some reasonable attempt at care can be made.

Now we need to examine the skills and competencies required in staff caring for customers and then reflect on how these can be better delivered to new or existing staff.

We live in times of increasing consumer sophistication. Times of recession highlight the need to provide value-for-money care if companies are to survive, and customers now seek and demand both excellent service and quality, generally at the 'delivery' level, that is, the face-to-face contact point.

To receive satisfaction, customers expect to receive consistently good service all of the time and to have their expectations exceeded some of the time! Remember, 'When my treatment is less than my expectations – that is bad service'; When my treatment is more than my expectations – that is good service'. Also, bad news always travels further and faster than any other. The average dissatisfied customer will tell at least 10 people about poor goods and service, while 1 in 5 will tell as many as 20 ('Customer Complaint Handling in America', TARP, 1980, Final Report Washington DC White House Office of Consumer Affairs). Upset one customer on a 53-seater coach on a package holiday and it is easy to see the outcome (we have all seen how bad news spreads on a railway station or in an airport lounge!)

The importance of front-line staff, therefore, cannot be overemphasized and, yet, little research has been undertaken on what sorts of skills and competencies they need to have – from both the staff's and the customer's point of view. That is until 1988, when a study undertaken by Dr Richard Wellins and Wendy Becker ('Analysing Customer Service Perceptions', Development Dimensions International, 1988) produced valuable evidence not only regarding the main skills and competencies expected of staff in contact with and caring for customers but also of the different perceptions of these skills by staff and customers.

After an extensive search of available literature and analysis of staff jobs with customer contact elements, 9 service skills and 17 competencies were identified as being the essential ingredients for care positions and, ultimately, the ingredients for any customer care training programme. Subsequently checked by job experts, the following nine skill areas were concluded to be very important:

1 *make the customer feel important* by greeting courteously, showing concern for their needs, asking the right questions, giving compliments
2 *listening and responding* particularly to feelings or moods, attempting to establish *empathy* with the customer to achieve satisfaction
3 *asking and offering* getting interest, creating conversation, reassessment when customer is overawed or uncertain
4 *quickly acknowledging* using the customer's name when possible, giving full attention, adjusting to the mood or pace of the customer once a response has been given
5 *clarify details* ask effective questions, get all the details, give out all the essential information clearly
6 *exceed, rather than simply meet, demands* work to solve problems, suggest additional services, go out of the way to be helpful
7 *ensure satisfaction* ask, check, ask, then check again that the customer is satisfied before saying 'Goodbye'
8 *prepare* know the job, the products, the services, have everything needed for the job available, be well-groomed and attentive, be trained regularly
9 *follow-up* call back or follow up with information, keep everyone informed, work with others to maintain communications, and ensure customer satisfaction.

This is quite a list, but a valuable one when it comes to planning training sessions and when ensuring, operationally, that all care staff have received the necessary information to give to the customers. A phrase that might apply to all nine might be 'keeping one jump ahead'!

It also means knowing both what a customer *wants* and *needs*. He *wants* a meal in a restaurant, service at a trade counter, knowledge and results over a telephone; he *needs* quick service, expertise, clear, sharp instructions.

The 17 competencies – categories of behaviour, and very important ingredients to training programmes – Wellins and Becker produced were the following:

1 *communication* being able to clearly express oneself when communicating with customers (verbal or written), with no recourse to jargon
2 *being customer-sensitive* recognizing and showing concern for customers needs or feelings or points of view
3 *being decisive* taking action or making quick decisions that address customers' needs – in other words, don't dither or blame someone else
4 *have energy* being alert and attentive, playing a major role on the front stage
5 *being flexible* able to quickly change a service style, action or approach to meet a perceived need, personality or disposition, but still remain within the company's standards and rules
6 *follow-up* delivers what has been promised or committed on time and according to the order
7 *makes an impact* a neat appearance, firm bearing, and creates a positive impression on the customer
8 *has initiative* consistently tries to meet or exceed the customer's expectations, to be 'one jump ahead'
9 *has integrity* is open, honest, and ethical, makes no false promises, lets neither the customer, colleagues nor company down
10 *has job knowledge* shows a thorough understanding of a company's products and services as well as the policy or procedure for customer care
11 *has judgement* uses available information to address and solve customers' problems, utililizes some empowerment, thinks for themselves to meet needs
12 *is motivated to serve* gains job satisfaction and fulfilment from serving or dealing with customers, meeting their needs or handling concerns – not quite born to it, but certainly pleased to perform
13 *is persuasive* moving a competence in care into the 'selling mode', which entails not only obtaining customer acceptance of the solutions to problems, but also convincing them of the benefits of a company's products and services
14 *plans* prepares and organizes the work so there is time to talk to the customers and a readiness to cope with reactions
15 *resilient* most jobs involving customer contact require patience and tact; there will be an element of unpredictability regarding what is a priority

for a particular customer and a need to withstand the pressures and overcome the problems, so it follows that looking after customers calls for
good health and fitness

16 *can analyse and react* if things go wrong (which they do) can gather relevant
information and facts about a situation, analyse what the best solution will
be, then react, plan, and organize a solution to everyone's benefit

17 *has standards* knows, establishes, and maintains high standards of customer care and service, striving always to achieve them or exceed them.

Another impressive list. It is perhaps not surprising that few really achieve all
of them, all of the time (Figure 5.1). A fact borne out by the remainder of Wellins
and Becker's research. In this they asked customers and staff in contact with
customers to rate each skill or competence in terms of importance (5 =
extremely important, 1 = not important) and how well done it was (5 = always,
1 = never). The results for both aspects show big differences in the scores.

Table 5.1 shows clearly the distinction between the importance placed on the
nine skills by the customers and how well each is achieved. Table 5.2 shows a
similar difference in relation to the 17 competencies.

**Figure 5.1 Staff, though not perfect, need to try to display particular
competencies in order to give quality service**

Table 5.1 Wellins and Becker's list of skill areas with ratings given by customers

Skills	Importance	How well done
1 Make the customer feel important	4.09	2.90
2 Listening and responding to customer's feelings	4.07	2.72
3 Asking for ideas and offering suggestions	3.62	2.72
4 Acknowledging the customer	3.86	2.91
5 Clarify details about the situation	3.84	2.70
6 Meet (or exceed) customers' demands	4.02	2.72
7 Ensure customer is satisfied	3.99	2.81
8 Prepare	4.18	2.92
9 Follow-up	4.01	2.57

Table 5.2 Wellins and Becker's list of competencies with ratings given by customers

Skills	Importance	How well done
Communication	4.05	2.95
Being customer-sensitive	3.92	2.69
Being decisive	3.84	2.74
Have energy	3.87	2.89
Being flexible	3.71	2.68
Follow-up	4.09	2.68
Makes an impact	3.80	3.24
Has initiative	3.67	2.54
Has integrity	3.97	2.87
Has job knowledge	4.10	2.96
Has judgement	3.82	2.80
Is motivated to serve	3.97	2.73
Is persuasive	3.56	2.91
Plans	3.76	2.74
Resilient	3.84	2.75
Can analyse and react	3.71	2.77
Has standards	3.93	2.81

For those staff in contact with customers a much higher mark is placed on each skill and competence area (see Tables 5.3 and 5.4), with a similar higher mark for how well each is achieved. From all this information can be gleaned one salutary fact: staff think they are doing far better at caring than their customers do!

The research attempted to rate the skills and competencies in some order of importance, and achieved a fair degree of agreement as a result. A feeling of importance and acknowledgement produced high votes in the skills, while judgement and follow-up scored highly in the competencies. What is not in doubt is the *content* of these skills and competencies and, therefore, their importance in training and customer care development programmes. In essence, five main strands emerge. These are:

● *common sense* an ability to think clearly and plan ahead – as well as review afterwards – and think on one's feet in an emergency

● *good relationships* between the server, their manager, and the customer, including trust, integrity, making judgements, and building up support in order to perform effectively

● *a natural ability* including dress sense, speech, bearing, even poise and charm – in essence, something of an actor, putting on a daily or hourly show

● *good job knowledge* in order to be able to make judgements and decisions, plan effectively with clear boundaries of control

● *communications* perhaps the most vital, providing the channels to speak, write and show in a non-verbal way how best to serve the needs of the customer.

Table 5.3 Wellins and Becker's list of skill areas with ratings given by staff

Skills	Importance	How well done
1 Make the customer feel important	4.55	3.62
2 Listening and responding to customer's feelings	4.52	3.56
3 Asking for ideas and offering suggestions	3.79	3.06
4 Acknowledging the customer	4.31	3.71
5 Clarify details about the situation	4.49	3.59
6 Meet (or exceed) customers' demands	4.44	3.43
7 Ensure customer is satisfied	4.31	3.51
8 Prepare	4.55	3.53
9 Follow-up	4.54	3.35

Table 5.4 Wellins and Becker's list of competencies with ratings given by staff

Competencies	Importance	How well done
Communication	4.55	3.64
Being customer-sensitive	4.38	3.56
Being decisive	4.34	3.53
Have energy	4.21	3.38
Being flexible	4.20	3.47
Follow-up	4.51	3.31
Makes an impact	3.84	3.66
Has initiative	4.00	3.13
Has integrity	4.29	3.64
Has job knowledge	4.54	3.56
Has judgement	4.31	3.59
Is motivated to serve	4.27	3.32
Is persuasive	4.03	3.23
Plans	4.05	3.24
Resilient	4.32	3.42
Can analyse and react	4.26	3.55
Has standards	4.26	3.44

These skills and competencies are fully reflected in the five units of competence required from candidates working for an NVQ in customer service (see Figure 5.2). Assessed at Level 3, the Supervisor Level, the RSA-devised NVQ requires a thorough understanding of the following to be demonstrated:

1 *maintaining reliable customer service* including records and organization of work
2 *communication with customers* different methods and flows
3 *developing positive working relationships with customers* by responding to needs and feelings, presenting a personal image, and balancing customers' and organizational needs
4 *solving customers' problems by identifying what needs to be done and taking action*
5 *initiating and evaluating changes to improve service* communicating and contributing to evaluation of service and then acting on the results.

Figure 5.2 Candidate for NVQ being assessed in customer service

Again it must be noted how important *communication* is – indeed, it features across all the assessment criteria for the award.

Finally, the skills and competencies are a useful aid to the recruitment of staff (and the ideal person specification) described in Chapter 4.

In summary, there is a need for well-dressed, quick-thinking communicators, who are able to get on well with people, making them feel important, but also able to contribute not only as individuals, but as team members. Don't hide such people away, behind drab uniforms, show them off, give them name badges, allow them to build up a rapport with the customers, producing loyalty, commitment, and all-round satisfaction. In other words, find the right people for the job!

Training and operational activities

• •

1 MANAGEMENT

Hand copies of Tables 5.5 and 5.6 to the management team concerned with customer contacts, and ask them to study them carefully. Ask them to:

● list all those skills and competencies needed by staff in the company

● grade the skills and competencies in order of importance

● grade the skills and competencies in the order in which they are currently performed by their staff (and themselves) – using the blank tables.

ask them to carry out this audit individually and compare the results.

The skills and competencies tables are those produced by Wellins and Becker's research, but here, the ratings have been removed. Have the management team give a rating of 1 (lowest) to 5 (highest) for each skill or competence, both for its importance and how well done it is in *their* company.

If it is not already in operation, construct a feedback questionnaire to give to customers or guests that will be easy to use, quick to complete, and provide all the details you require to check on the skills and elements of care provided in your establishment. (This may be used to supplement the questionnaires discussed in Chapter 4.)

If such a questionnaire is already in use, examine it again in the light of this chapter. Does it pinpoint any lack of skill or competence in staff or management? If not, adjust it so that you can quickly highlight such problems and provide the necessary training.

2 STAFF

As for the first exercise, make copies of tables 5.5 and 5.6, but this time circulate them to all staff in positions involving customer contact. Compare the results with those produced by the managers in a joint session.

Table 5.5 Wellins and Becker's list of skill areas

Skills	Importance	How well done
1 Make the customer feel important		
2 Listening and responding to customer's feelings		
3 Asking for ideas and offering suggestions		
4 Acknowledging the customer		
5 Clarify details about the situation		
6 Meet (or exceed) customers' demands		
7 Ensure customer is satisfied		
8 Prepare		
9 Follow-up		

Table 5.6 Wellins and Becker's list of competencies

Competencies	Importance	How well done
Communication		
Being customer-sensitive		
Being decisive		
Have energy		
Being flexible		
Follow-up		
Makes an impact		
Has initiative		
Has integrity		
Has job knowledge		
Has judgement		
Is motivated to serve		
Is persuasive		
Plans		
Resilient		
Can analyse and react		
Has standards		

Take more copies of Tables 5.5 and 5.6 and ask your regular customers to rate the skills and competencies for themselves and then how well each skill or competence is carried out by your staff or managers in their opinion. Again, compare the results of all the sets of tables.

Using the check-list overleaf, have staff observe all customer contact points over a period of time. (Not continuously, but in short, controlled bursts at busy, quiet or difficult times.)

Check that staff know what kinds of activities indicate that these skills or competencies are being exercised. Once the observations have been completed, it will be possible to clearly identify both individual shortcomings and the general performance of each one. The results will provide the basis for general or individual training sessions (some suggestions for such training are given on the right-hand side of the check-list).

Note It is likely that several *operational* defects may become apparent during the course of this exercise, such as a badly sited reception desk, too much paperwork needs to be done for staff to be able to provide the best service, there are too few staff to cover peak times, and so on. If this is the case, action may be necessary. Training will not automatically solve problems; other action may need to be taken. The 'Comments' column can be used to note any such need for action.

CHECKLIST OF SKILLS AND COMPETENCIES		
Skills	*Comments*	*Training methods*
1 Greeting Show interest. Be welcoming – smile, etc. Show concern for customer.		Role plays. Raise confidence level by giving assertiveness training.
2 Listening/responding Watch reaction to requests. Give right answer to questions. Know details of company.		Body language training. Proper induction. Staff handbook.
3 Ask/offer Start conversation, using name. Offer reassurance or support – put at ease.		Confidence in product knowledge – role plays, manner of response training through case studies.
4 Acknowledge Respond quickly when busy/not busy. Use name when known. Adjust pace to suit customers, even when busy, particularly for those with special needs/disabled.		Role plays, knowledge of records. Recognition of needs. Response training through case studies.
5 Clarify details Repeat back information politely. Give correct information. Show care in dealings/conversation.		Product/procedure knowledge. Handling difficult people, training (role plays).
6 Exceed/meet demand Find out how difficulties can be overcome. Sell up other services/products. Meet every reasonable demand.		Knowledge of full range of products. Handling difficult/crisis situations.

Skills	Comments	Training methods
7 Ensure satisfaction Ask, check, smile, confirm, say farewell. Use name, write up records.		General care training. Record-keeping details training.
8 Prepare Ready before time, fully prepared with necessary information. Well-dressed/groomed, alert, attentive.		Proper induction. Uniform care, take no stress/moods to work, etc.
9 Follow-Up Follow through problems, and report to customer/manager. Check shortcomings have been sorted out.		Confidence in job and product. Ease with customer. Organization chart, communications map.

Competencies	Comments	Training methods
1 Communication Clear, accurate information given. No jargon used. Helps with foreign (non-English speaking) customers.		Communication and listening skills course. Product knowledge.
2 Customer-sensitive Show genuine concern for each individual (however busy). Treat as most important. Smile. Eye contact established.		Communication and listening skills course. Body language knowledge. Role plays.
3 Decisive Take right action quickly to meet customer requests. Know job/authority/responsibility and chain of command.		Assertiveness, product knowledge, chain of communication/authority.

Competencies	Comments	Training methods
4 Energy Like an actor, alert, playing a part, ready for any crisis.		Natural ability; know where to go if problems occur (induction).
5 Flexible Adjust performance to needs of customer – read situation and respond appropriately. Maintain company standards of care.		Company performance standards. Role plays. Product knowledge and limits of authority.
6 Follow-Up Take each request to its conclusion. Ensure others know situation and check.		Company procedure. Teamwork programme.
7 Make an impact Bearing, appearance, stance. All-welcoming, not intimidating. Positive responses every time.		Grooming, uniform, voice production. Role plays.
8 Initiative Know limits of authority and work within these to customers' benefit. Try to anticipate needs.		Job role, product knowledge. Build-up of experience.
9 Integrity No lies or false promises. Work with team – open and honest. Company/team loyalty.		Job knowledge, team building – incentives.

Competencies	Comments	Training methods
10 Job knowledge Know all products, services and procedures and provide clear information.		Test job knowledge by questionnaire.
11 Judgement Think on feet. Know what to do, when to solve a customer's problem. Practice empowerment where necessary.		Job responsibilities and limits of authority.
12 Motivated Like people and show it. Active, pleasant manner with customers and team members.		Length of service incentives; correct recruitment.
13 Persuasive Sell up, but not too hard. Suggest alternatives.		Job knowledge.
14 Planning Well-prepared and organized at all times – give time so customers not rushed or hurried.		Job knowledge and length of service.
15 Resilience Show patience, tact, and diplomacy. No temper or stress; react calmly under pressure.		Assertiveness training. Natural ability. Job knowledge.

Competencies	Comments	Training methods
16 Analysis and reaction Gathers relevant facts to explain difficulties. Use information to do better next time. Do not let customer down.		Role plays and case studies. Records; job knowledge.
17 Have standards Know job well, maintain correct level at all times, including customer rules.		Care standards training.

Role plays

To back up the training suggested in the check-list, here are a series of role plays to use as necessary.

☞ Role play 1

Customer

You are idly looking at some pocket calculators in a local shop close to where you are attending a conference (your name badge is still on your jacket). You have it in mind to purchase one, but you aren't sure which is the best value for money. An assistant approaches and offers to help. Within seconds, they are calling you by your name and showing great enthusiasm for the products on display. You listen but are determined *not* to buy.

Staff

You are an assistant in the small electrical section of a local store near a hotel. Your particular expertise is pocket calculators. You see a would-be purchaser looking at the stock and approach. They have a name badge on, so you assume they are attending a conference at the hotel and get into a conversation. You are determined to make a sale.

☞ Role play 2

Customer

You are in a major hurry to catch a train for an important meeting. There is a queue in front of you at the booking office and the person in front of you has a time-consuming query about train times. You try to interrupt, but the booking clerk looks at you and says 'wait your turn'. Eventually, your turn comes and they seem to be dealing with your ticket very slowly. Your temper rises.

Staff

It is a busy day in the booking office – new season tickets, a new timetable, so many queries . . . you become aware, while dealing with a nice old lady wanting train information, that an irate person is trying to barge in. Their turn comes, but, because of new fares, and so on, you have to take your time. Flashpoint approaches, you feel.

☞ *Role play 3*

Staff

You are working behind the bar of a very busy pub. There are several big parties and you have to carefully check with those ordering to ensure that correct drinks are provided. Then, you spot a regular behind several faces at the bar. They can be difficult if kept waiting. Take it from here.

Customers

Use several trainees to play drinkers and one to play the difficult regular who wants quick service. Use this role play to check how trainees clarify details or deal with 'acknowledging' when they are busy or cope with difficult customers.

☞ *Role play 4*

Customer

However hard you try, there is something about the corner shop that gets your back up. You go there regularly for cigarettes and a paper, but whether it is the untidiness, muddle or the overpleasant assistants, you normally end up being a little rude. Today may be no exception.

Staff

It is about the right time for one of your very regular customers to come into your small, overcrowded, and chaotic shop for a newspaper and cigarettes. You try hard to please, you know them well, but, practically every day, some argument or nasty remark is made. Today could be the same (or different?).

☞ *Role play 5*

Customer

You approach an assistant at the Tourist Information Centre to enquire about tickets for a local concert. They are normally very efficient and friendly and today, initially, is no exception. You ask your question, but realize by the 'eyes down' look and the other body language that they are unable to help you as normal – what can you do to help.

Staff

You work in the local Tourist Information Centre, which also handles local concert and other bookings. Today, one of your regulars comes in to book tickets for a concert about which you have no information, but which doesn't sound like their sort of thing at all! You try to cover your lack of knowledge and disapproval, but find this difficult. Use lack of eye contact and other body language – move away, fold your arms, and so on – to show this.

Observers

They need to watch what happens to the rest of this role play which should be done by good 'actors'. Learning the lessons about how lack of knowledge or a display of feelings can affect care transactions.

Case studies

These can be used to reinforce any training suggested in the check-list.

FLEXIBILITY

You are the Manager of a local DIY store. On this particular day, you first receive a call from a supervisor informing you that they have disciplined one of the part-time staff for not applying company standards when helping a customer.

Apparently, the member of staff spent a long time trying to help an elderly customer who couldn't decide on a particular drill. Several other customers were kept waiting and a lot of boxes and packaging were damaged as a result of opening so many to demonstrate the different types.

You agree to mark the file, but, a few minutes later, the member of staff concerned (who is keen and efficient) comes up to your office to explain. They are very upset about the incident and, after some discussion, a threat of resignation is made.

Staff are very hard to find at present and you don't want to lose them, but company rules have to be kept to. You end the discussion by saying you will consider it and see them later.

An hour later, a telephone call is taken from the elderly customer who says how delighted they are with their purchase of just the right drill and asking for their thanks to be passed on to the member of staff who helped them.

What are you to do? Back the Supervisor or praise the staff member for their enthusiasm, flexibility and the fact that they achieved a sale, even though company rules were abused?

Your task

As Manager decide what you have to tell the Supervisor (in the light of the customer's telephone call) and how you will handle the member of staff at the second meeting. Also, how will you ensure that the Supervisor and staff will continue to work together.

Analysis and reaction

Miss James is an occasional caller at the Springfield Inn, a well-known restaurant and bar in a small, country village.

On her birthday, she invites a few friends for a meal and drink at the Inn. Here she meets a new member of staff who doesn't know her and is rather off-hand. Her favourite sherry is not available, the bar is crowded and smoky, and Miss James feels very let down.

Before going in to eat, she confronts the member of staff and complains about her service and how she has been embarrassed in front of her friends.

Some weeks later, her cousin comes to stay and takes her into the Springfield Inn. At first she is reluctant to enter, but succumbs.

On reaching the bar, the same member of staff immediately recognizes her, calls her by name and, without asking, pours her a glass of her favourite sherry, and refuses to charge for it.

Your task

To explore and explain what might have happened between the two visits (in line with competency 16). Draw out the importance of analysing shortcomings or complaints and how easy it can be to correct past mistakes.

Tutor's note

It is suggested that staff involved in customer care be urged to take the RSA Level 3 NVQ in Customer Service, as in the course of this, they will be properly assessed against the performance criteria for each unit by trained assessors from within the company.

6

....

WHAT CAN
GO WRONG

INTRODUCTION

We have examined all the positive sides of care, so now we need to turn the coin over and look at how or why things go wrong.

Everyone has a bad customer care story to tell. Generally they are connected with transport – British Rail being a typical target – as well as motorway services, telephone answering, the Post Office or the classic retail experience!

Take a moment to remember one of your own experiences, then try to analyse what happened and why. The chances are that the reasons will fit into one of the 'big five 'C's' described in this chapter, probably aided and abetted by one or more of the difficulties discussed later, such as appearance, assumption, mood or stress.

It may include no welcoming procedure, poor service, lack of product knowledge, bad communications. Ultimately, what will happen is the *opposite* of good customer care. You should now 'put yourself in the *carer's* shoes' to work out why it all went wrong!

Good care and service is a highly skilled activity, requiring a high level of commitment and competence. It also requires some imagination and *supportive management*. If good care fails to work, then one or more of the following has probably happened.

'THE BIG FIVE 'C'S'

The first can be a *lack of commitment*. Providing service and care is hard work, requiring, as we have learned, patience, tact, and skill. It also requires a great deal of *involvement* with the customer (remember CICC – page 6). This means ensuring that personnel in contact with customers are not put under too much pressure to succeed, that their problems are listened to and suggestions acted upon, and that working conditions are made as pleasant as possible so that there is sufficient time and encouragement to build up the commitment to the customer's care and needs.

A lack of commitment is manifested in many ways: a look of boredom, a poor welcome, a *laissez-faire* attitude, listlessness, or lifelessness behind a desk, being late to come on duty, quick to take time off, argumentative, badly turned out, and not at all interested in putting the customer first.

The second 'C' is *lack of confidence*. No one can care for a customer well if they lack confidence in either their managers, supervisors or company backing up and supporting them. Worse, perhaps, is a lack of confidence in the products they are 'selling' as well as a lack of confidence in what has to be done.

Confidence will always falter if a company is going through hard times, if a takeover is imminent, if redundancies threaten. Only the best players (literally acting out a part) will show some confidence in these circumstances; the rest are bound to suffer a crisis of confidence, and customer care will be the loser. A vicious circle ensues: poor care equals fewer customers equals less profit equals more chance of failure.

Care is not only about being nice to people, it is also all about being helpful. Providing help means knowing *all about* the company and the products, so that every question can be answered.

A lack of confidence in staff involved in customer care is easy to see. The eyes look down when a difficult question is asked, they have to go and ask someone else – leaving the customer in the lurch – they make strange excuses, do not know the features or benefits of a product, give the wrong information, keep customers waiting on the telephone, and so on.

The secrets of instilling confidence are down to good training, effective follow-up, and workable systems. Staff need to be:

● properly prepared for anything, have an idea about the questions customers ask and the answers to give them

● knowledgeable about the products, the range, the service, the distribution – in other words, everything the company provides

● conversant with all the internal procedures for achieving the best service – rules, regulations, standards – and, very important – what authority is available to them to make adjustments to these standards to benefit the customer

● able to turn to someone else if help is needed, to feel that they are not on their own in a crisis, when the totally unexpected might happen.

This last point leads us neatly on to the third 'C' – *lack of cooperation*. Although, in the end, care comes down to customer and staff undertaking a one-to-one conversation, back-up for the staff is a *team* of people in whom that front person has confidence. As has been shown, we are all customers of each other, so all those operating in the service side have a piece of the jigsaw to fit into the whole picture that contributes to making the whole perform effectively. If one lets the system down, the picture is incomplete, a nasty gap ensues, and care of the customer suffers.

Today it is fashionable to blame technology for any shortcomings in the care process: 'Your invoice has been missed off the last run', 'The order didn't go through', 'We didn't receive the details of your arrival in time', and so on. All are plausible excuses, perhaps, yet the computer is operated by a *member of the team*. They have to realize what results from their inefficiency, the effect it has not only on the customers but also on the poor member of staff either facing them or telephoning them.

Typical symptoms of such a lack of cooperation, apart from the aforementioned 'technological' excuses are those that involve saying that someone else should have done 'X' but didn't – 'The previous shift didn't complete all the work', 'We didn't know about your special order', 'We are short of staff', and, perhaps worst of all, 'It's not my job'!

By far the greatest of the five 'lacks' is *lack of communication*, and it is generally the one most blamed for care breakdowns. Despite the fact that, as human beings, we have the priceless gift of being able to talk to each other, write letters or simply communicate via signs and signals, there are far too many instances of messages not getting through or wrong meanings being attributed to instructions or simple care contacts.

However hard one tries, there appears to be no simple answer to this problem. The communication map of Chapter 2 will provide the route, but it will not solve the difficulty of a key staff member forgetting a message, a customer receiving the wrong one or a total muddle ensuing because written instructions go to the wrong place.

Moreover, the trouble, perhaps, is that it is easy to blame communications for all our problems: 'It's not me it's the system', 'I told him to do it and he hasn't'. When in doubt, of course, we hide behind myriad forms of jargon, developing a capital letter syndrome to hide the fact that something hasn't been done: 'Your letter was read by the DOM and passed to our CSE department, they instructed the SM to reply but he is off sick'!

There is no easy answer for this lack, which, of course, includes poor handwriting, unclear instructions, and a lack of understanding in addition to simply not giving a clear answer to the poor customer. In many ways, it is inherent in the other lacks. If staff are confident or committed they will communicate better with regard to customers' needs. If the team functions effectively, communications will be better. Above all, the message to managers should be, *never blame poor communications for a lack of care*.

The last of the lacks is just this – a *lack of care*. This is not just a complete résumé of all that has gone before, but, more important, the old message that good *staff* care equals good *customer* care. If staff are happy in their jobs, feel appreciated, are given the opportunity to perform and a chance to contribute to their own well-being, they will pass on this contentment to the customers with whom they are in contact. This does not mean that money should be thrown at the problem by increasing salaries (although this will help), but, rather, that the facilities, welfare, openness, and care to which they as human beings are entitled should be provided for them. Remember we are all customers of each other.

Again, this 'C' is linked, in part, to the other big five C's because good communications and teamwork will provide commitment, confidence, and therefore, care.

The symptoms of poor staff care are easy to spot. A high labour turnover among all staff in contact with customers at all levels, too much dependence on autocracy, no discussions before decisions are taken that affect everyone. Late arrivals, early departures, greater 'sickness' absence, a flourishing grapevine of rumour – often associated with poor communication and lack of care – and a general attitude of non-caring – 'Why should I bother about the firm's customer if they don't bother about me'!

So far, we have discussed the personal aspects of what can go wrong from more of a teamwork angle, most of which can be solved by training and better communication. There are, though, two other elements that have to be considered. These are:

- operational difficulties
- the individual's own attitude to care and the customer.

OPERATIONAL DIFFICULTIES

It is often an easy trap to fall into when dealing with care in a service environment (people-to-people) to think that *all* problems can be solved by talking, training or simply revamping the communication process. However, there are many instances where it is the operational procedure, the equipment in use or the rules and regulations that need to change rather then the people.

A good example is having a telephone switchboard operating only from 9.00 am –5.00 pm in an export-related company that deals with many overseas calls. While this may not be a problem initially, it quickly becomes one if the Marketing Department has no means of dialling direct or receiving calls after 5.00 pm.

Another is having so many rules or red tape connected with care for the customer that the staff are reluctant to use the system. Why, for example, should it cost £5 in staff time, letter writing, receipt signing, and a general lack of trust, to refund £1 to a customer? Simply empowering staff at the front line and using a single form would save time, money, and effort and, ultimately, probably reduce refunds to a tiny trickle!

We are gradually waking up to these facts within industry, with charters and codes of practice having some effect, but there is still some reluctance to sweep away bureaucracy entirely – the triplicate form still lives! As part of any drive to improve customer care, it is essential to look carefully at all the operational procedures where customers come into contact with the company system and examine really how efficient the system is.

THE INDIVIDUALS

We now come to perhaps the hardest part of all in this chapter – ourselves!

Prejudices

What do we really think of our neighbours, our customers, our team mates? Do we show our feelings openly or subconsciously through our body language? What are our prejudices?

It is also hard because so many assumptions or prejudices are inherent in our upbringing, education or family background. The carer thinks that what they are saying or doing is perfectly natural; the customer, however, may be scandalized or deeply offended by an attitude, a throwaway remark or a certain look.

We have also to consider the difficult question of body language. However hard we try to hide our feelings, our subconscious is reacting differently, so we turn away, look down, fold our arms or give a 'don't trust you' look to our customer.

Their own subconscious reacts to this and an immediate lack of trust or dislike can be the result. Such reactions are most prevalent regarding the usual discriminations of race, colour, sex, and disability, together, still, with religion.

Other prejudices that can come to the surface include:

● *appearance* how a customer actually looks in terms of dress, cleanliness or bearing affects how we treat them (see Figure 6.1)

● *voice* accents and language affect our dealings with people, so, if they are foreign, we may slow down our speech, start to shout, talk in a 'pidgin English' way and subconsciously show our frustration at having to take longer over the transaction, while a 'country accent' in an urban environment still can induce an element of 'slowness' into the conversation

● *context* we tend to associate people with places and how they are dressed or what they are doing may be different to what we expect, which tends to alter the sort of care we provide, and if remarks are made about this ('You are all dressed up today'), they may insult or offend our customer or draw attention to something they want to forget.

Putting all this right is hard and requires careful handling – plenty of practise away from the front desk, and a very open and frank environment in which to discuss attitudes, assumptions, and prejudices.

Figure 6.1 Prejudices regarding appearance can affect the care we give particular customers

Moods

All of us at some point are likely to experience work and private pressures that will affect the way we perform our jobs. The problem, often, is that the resulting mood is taken out on the customer, particularly if they are being slow or difficult.

The obvious way to avoid such problems is to provide a happy working environment for staff involved with customer care and an opportunity to talk over problems as necessary, with someone who is good at listening and has some useful advice. Obviously this is not a professional counsellor but a friendly 'ear'.

An easy cure for a mood is to remember that front-line staff are actually on a stage, as it were, performing to their customers – their audience. If the mood or bad temper is not to be spotted, an Oscar-winning performance may have to be given! It is essential, though, to leave moods behind in the changing room, taking them back (hopefully cured after a change of activity) after the shift has been completed.

Stress

Moods often lead to or are the result of stress. Stress, though, is often caused by poor working practices, a shortage of staff or overbearing supervision. To relieve stress – like curing moods – quick but effective action is required if it is not to lead to a far more serious condition, like depression.

The demands made by customers on members of staff or managers easily cause stress and annoyance, so, to avoid it, here are six suggestions:

1 *work at a steady pace* not rushing about in a disorganized way, which, of course, means ensuring that the work pattern is properly assessed with adequate staff and efficient systems being put in place to cope with it
2 *exercise regularly* provide some form of sport or recreational facility
3 *talk over problems* have a friendly ear available to relieve the tensions of dealing with people by talking about situations and so on
4 *eat well* to have sufficient energy and stay healthy – how good are the staff meals?
5 *take moments to relax* this is particularly important after handling difficult situations, so sufficient staff need to be provided to allow for this
6 *ensure staff have plenty of rest and sleep* the challenges of each day can be great, so double shifts and excessive overtime do *not* create a good care environment.

Time

This is not a Time Management book, but this principal is a useful one in relation to care. Good care takes a lot of time, particularly when staff are ensuring that customers are happy, satisfied, understand the procedure or the answer to a question or problem, and that they leave feeling properly looked after (pampered!) Having no time is an easy excuse, but it can mean that the customer has been lost to someone else, who does have time to care.

Time must be made for care but not too much – remember, the customer has limited time also! Allow sufficient time to listen (not assuming but understanding what's wanted), then take action, carrying out what's wanted effectively. If a customer has to ask again, you may have failed to care properly!

Time Management of care – procedures, systems, responsibilities – are, therefore, just as important as the smile of welcome.

Training and operational activities

· ·

STAFF

Why do organizations lose customers? (Welcome host exercise, English Tourist Board, 1993*) Table 6.1 shows the seven main reasons for this. Ask staff to estimate the percentages that go in the blank spaces (they should total 100).

Table 6.1 Why do organizations lose customers?

Percentage Reason	Answers
_____ % of customers die.	1%
_____ % of customers move away.	3%
_____ % of customers float from one company to another.	4%
_____ % of customers change firms because of a friend's recommendation.	7%
_____ % of customers stop dealing with companies because staff are indifferent or show little interest.	68%
_____ % of customers are chronic complainers.	8%
_____ % of customers change because they can buy more cheaply elsewhere.	9%

The main purpose of this exercise is to pinpoint the large number of customers who don't return because of staff indifference (commitment). It is likely that few staff will get all the percentages correct. Lead a discussion on the results and take note of any special comments from staff that can be actioned.

*Source: Ministry of Tourism, Province of British Columbia, Canada.

Confidence questionnaire

Construct a number of 'What if . . . ?' questions for staff to answer, either verbally or in writing. Here are some examples.

● Your supervisor is away sick, and the senior member of staff is on a break when a customer comes in with a particularly difficult problem (such as a complaint about faulty goods that may affect their consumer rights). They are in a hurry, but require an answer. What would you do?

● You are answering the telephone in a customer service capacity, you have been told always to 'sell up' when giving answers so that the customer is encouraged to buy more. What would you go for and how would you do it (using a product or a service)?

● A customer rings up asking for details of the company rules regarding the return of goods – they purchased something from you three days ago. What is your reply?

● You are alone in the office of a bus company, which always insists on a written application for refunds to passengers, together with the reason for its being requested. A passenger walks in claiming that his bus never arrived and he had to get a taxi in order to reach the bus station to catch a coach to the airport. He is going abroad for six months and wants cash now. The fare was £1.30. How would you deal with him?

● You have just started work in your retail department when a rather belligerent customer walks in to complain about the attitude of one of the part-time staff yesterday (they are not on duty today). Your supervisor is coming in late after a dental appointment. The customer is beginning to shout and demand action. What do you say?

● Your telephone rings. A customer, who has a very bad line, is trying to give you a message about the non-delivery of some goods. You cannot get the name or the full address, despite asking them to repeat it twice, but you manage to find out what *was* to be delivered before the line goes dead. Unfortunately, the actual item is one of several due for delivery that day to at least six people. What do you do?

Using all your company's products and services, produce a questionnaire that thoroughly tests the knowledge of the staff. Try to cover products, regulations, procedures, names of key personnel, and so on. This to provide *confidence* in the job. Ideally, 100 per cent should be the pass mark. Some examples of questions to test confidence and care are as follows.

- How many telephone rings should sound before the call is answered?

- The fire alarm sounds – what is your duty to the customers in your area?

- Our main product is .... Give three features and three benefits to mention when discussing it with a customer.

- You receive a complaint about a late delivery. Give the first five stages you would go through in placating the customer.

- Name three senior people in the company you can refer complaints or compliments to.

- You receive a letter asking for details of a product. What is the maximum/minimum time laid down for a reply to be sent?

- What is the company policy/procedure for acknowledging a customer on the shop floor?

- What is the minimum time before a customer should be acknowledged at the counter?

- How many main stock items are carried by .... department?

- Name your shift leader and deputy?

- A customer slips and falls while in the store. Describe what you have to do.

☞ Cooperation

Lead a discussion on how staff in contact with and caring for customers cooperate with others in the team. To assist, construct a number of possible scenarios that will test the knowledge of the company's products or service, distribution line, and managerial responsibilities (everyone is a customer of someone). Allow the discussions to broaden out so that it takes in some instances when teamwork failed. Again, use some 'What if . . . ?' scenarios such as the following.

- A letter is received, via the Manager, stating that someone in your department couldn't explain why some products were out of stock, and had been for several weeks. Your task is to write a reply explaining the ordering and distribution process and what has happened.

- You come on duty for the bar's evening shift to discover that those on duty earlier had failed to stock up the cold shelf and the 'bitter' line has also stopped working because the barrel hasn't been changed. Now customers are asking for cold beer. What can you do?

● As a hotel receptionist, your task is to show guests to their rooms. The Housekeeper has told you that Room 603 has been vacated and cleaned so you reallocate it to a new guest and escort them to the room. On arrival, the room clearly is still in a mess – the bed is unmade, dirty towels litter the floor, and there is a smell of stale cigar smoke. Unfortunately, the guest has *also* seen the room. What would you do?

● As the Company's Receptionist, you aim to ensure everyone receives a friendly welcome. Today, the person who cleans the outside area and the car park has been taken ill. One of your first visitors tells you that the car park is covered with pieces of paper dropped by a lorry changing next door's skip. What can you do?

Follow the discussions of these scenarious by drawing diagrams to show the team channels and where cooperation failed. Then, get the participants to suggest improvements and actions. Who is now going to work better with whom? What new system will be introduced to improve teamwork?

Communication

First, an often-used but effective training exercise designed to show the difference between one-way and two-way communication.

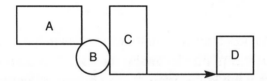

Figure 6.2 To be drawn on to card for 'volunteer' to describe without interacting with rest of group

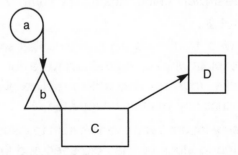

Figure 6.3 To be drawn on to card for 'volunteer' to describe interacting freely with rest of group

Figures 6.2 and 6.3 are both simple diagrams that can be drawn on to a piece of card. Give one 'volunteer' the first card (Figure 6.2) and, away from the rest of the group, brief them to describe what is on the card to everyone else. They will be facing the wall and will not be able to ask them any questions. Brief the group accordingly. They have to write down what they think has been described. Result: probably a 1 per cent success rate, frustration, some may give up, but it will be achieved quickly and quietly!

Next, hand Figure 6.3 to another volunteer, again briefing them in confidence. This time they will be in front of the group, and they can ask or answer questions and check progress, although the volunteer cannot show the card to the group. Brief the group and bring back the volunteer. Result: probably 90 per cent will achieve success and most of them will have asked a question to clarify the picture. As a result, all feel involved and happy to have achieved success, but it will have taken considerably longer to achieve.

Draw out from the group what's happened:

● *first effort* one-way communication – quick, no involvement, group switches off if lost, very inaccurate results, many failures, lack of understanding

● *second effort* two-way communication – took much longer, but everyone was fully involved, sense of achievement resulted, knew more what to expect, high success rate.

Lead a discussion on communications in care, with examples. Say, for one-way communication, a telephone message, written instructions, giving information with no checking, and so on. Two-way examples would be more thorough, such as involving face-to-face contact with two-way speech, questions to clarify, and so on. Link both to current company systems and discuss where improvements can be made.

Let us now look at the *process* of communication. Communication between people happens in three ways. Ask what these are. Answer:

● *verbal* with words
● *vocal* with words but with different emphases or tones
● *non-verbal* the mannerisms, body language, gesticulation.

Ask staff what percentages of the three make up the whole communication. Answer:

- words only, 10 per cent
- vocal, 35 per cent:
  - 'you *must* do it'
  - '*you* must do it' ⎫ examples of how tone and emphasis
  - 'you must *do* it' ⎬ alone can change meaning
  - 'you must do *it*' ⎭
- non-verbal, 55 per cent.

Explore the implications of this with the staff and how mannerisms and tone can totally alter the sense or meaning of a communication. For example, 'I am *so* pleased that you have arrived safely' may sound patronizing and insincere, if it is accompanied by no eye contact and the speaker moves away from the incoming customer!

Go over the skills that improve communication. These include:

- choosing the right time and place to communicate – you don't say that the restaurant has closed as the guest arrives
- use questions to check knowledge – 'How much do you know about our washing machine?'
- watch the receiver for non-verbal clues – frowning can mean a lack of understanding; stepping back means not interested
- always use simple words, two syllables rather than five, and no jargon – It will make it easier' rather than 'I can facilitate this for you'
- share your understanding of the message by repeating back – 'That's two coffees, one tea, and an orange juice'
- use a diagram or picture if necessary – fire escape notices, to clarify security; pointing directions when describing them for foreign customers
- use gestures to help – to portray size, direction, and so on, but be careful that they mean the same to everyone!

Listening is an important part of communication. We must remember, 'God gave us two ears and one mouth. We should listen twice as much as we speak'. As with the mnemonic WELCOME (Chapter 3), use the word LISTEN to bring home what communications should do to help listening. Get each person to think of at least two words or phrases beginning with the letters of the word 'listen'. For example,

L = look at, lean forward, learn, listen, language, level, like, lively, link

I = interest, interrupt (not), improve, ideas, identify, illustrate, image, imitate, impact, impair, impartial, impassive, impress, include, isolate

S = smile, satisfy, say nothing, silence, satisfy, sharp, sympathy, soothe, subconscious

T = tact, temper, teach, tread carefully, tell, tenacious, tense (not), test, thorough, thought (think), take time, total (commitment), transmit

E = empathy, enquire, ease, or easy, effort, ear, evoke, exclude (noise), express

N = neutralize (feelings), need, nice, natural, note, nudge, nurse, and (k)nowledge!

Ask staff to list as many words or uses of *jargon* operating in the company. Lead a discussion (and then take action) on how this can be avoided. Finally test the handwriting and communication skills of all staff in customer contact or care positions. Is it legible, could it lead to difficulties in communication? Point out the worst offenders and help them to correct/improve their writing, spelling or sentence construction.

Operations

Look into the provision of staff care – is it sufficient, does it give staff pride in the job, commitment, and therefore result in good care of customers?

How are problems of stress, mood or similar welfare difficulties coped with?

Are all the company's systems and operations involving customers 'customer friendly' – switchboard, notices, rules, procedures, and so on?

Are all the human resource systems geared up to cope with the identification of prejudice and solving cases of discrimination?

What sorts of assumptions are staff and managers making when dealing with customers?

Carry out some observations of staff at work and, if possible, set up some real-life tests to check their reactions to various typical problems. If possible, use video to watch their reactions.

You can use the following points to measure what is observed:

- attitude of staff behind a counter (rate on a scale from bored to enthusiastic)
- lengths of time to acknowledge customers (rate on a scale from three seconds to two minutes)
- standards of welcome – do they smile, acknowledge, find purpose, maintain interest, deal (SAPID) – and comment on the degree of genuineness
- if customers were kept waiting, what staff did – apologize, offer cup of coffee or tea, a seat, newspaper, or whatever
- handling of a late arrival
- handling of a complaint
- coping with a tricky problem
- how two or more members of staff worked together – signs of cooperation, back-up, and so on.

Role plays

Set up training sessions on prejudice, assumptions, and mood using some of the role plays that follow. There are others at the end of the book.

Because of the sensitive nature of some of the scenarios, only one side of a few of the role plays is provided. Trainers should use them carefully, ensuring that they are played out with as much genuine reaction as possible by the opposite party.

☞ Role play 1

You go for a job where your customer care skills are to be put to good use. Despite the advertisement, which implies the job is open to all, the interviewer makes it very obvious that they are looking only for a man/woman (which you choose will depend on the player chosen).

☞ Role play 2

Customer

You arrive at the hotel reception desk of an up-market country house hotel. You are tired, hungry, and rather dishevelled after a long journey. After greeting you formally, it becomes rather obvious that the Receptionist is showing all the signs of objecting to you being in the front hall, as if you are lowering the tone. You resolve to tackle the problem.

Staff

You are a Receptionist in an up-market country house hotel. A guest walks in looking extremely untidy, rather dirty, and rather aggressive. They don't look quite the sort of person your Manager says the hotel should encourage. Play it from there.

☞ *Role play 3*

Customer

A foreign visitor (and passport holder) to Britain, you go to a 'Bureau de Change' to obtain pounds in exchange for your own currency. Despite the fact that you speak fluent English, the assistant starts to speak very slowly and loudly at you. You play along with it a bit before your temper gets the better of you.

Staff

You are an assistant in a 'Bureau de Change'. It has been a hard day, with many non-English-speaking customers, several complaints. It's hot and it is nearly the end of your shift. This customer speaks with an accent, so you use your usual speak slowly/loudly routine until they suddenly lose their temper.

☞ *Role play 4*

Your boyfriend/girlfriend has left you, this morning, and you have already had an 'earful' from your Supervisor in the Service Department. You think you are catching 'flu and now this so-called customer is making racially abusive remarks to you while you stand behind the garage's reception desk. You've told them that their car isn't ready and how much it is likely to cost, but that hasn't made it any easier. Play it from there.

Case study

Use the following case study to aid traning.

MAKING ASSUMPTIONS

You come on duty at 7.00 am – the early shift at a busy reception desk of a 'close to the airport' hotel. You first duty is to check any messages left by the night shift and set up the remaining early calls operated automatically from your desk through the rooms' telephone extensions.

You are immediately plunged into work as an air crew are checking in after an overnight flight from the Middle East. At 7.15, you activate the wake-up system, and again at 7.30 for several rooms.

Work proceeds more peacefully until nearly 8.00 am when a guest rushes to the desk complaining that they were not woken and that they may now miss their flight. Several more similar cases are to follow, with two more now complaining that no taxis have been ordered.

Next, another guest refuses to pay their bill because they claim to have been grossly overcharged for their overnight snack. Things are becoming difficult. Then, the Manager arrives to try to placate all the complaints. While the Manager is talking to the guests, you find a note on the floor that has obviously fallen off the desk. It mentions problems with the wake-up system, advises switching to manual override, and asks you to book taxis for two guests!

The Manager is now asking you for an explanation. What can you say?

7

....

HANDLING COMPLAINTS AND OTHER MATTERS

INTRODUCTION

If all the advice provided in the previous chapters has not worked, it is likely that a complaint will be received from a customer, either personally, in writing or by telephone.

This chapter concentrates on dealing with such a situation and, because the written or telephoned complaint is, if anything more common than the face-to-face one, we talk also of the use of letters, brochures, and telephone calls in customer care.

THE 'A' WORDS AND HANDLING COMPLAINTS FACE-TO-FACE

Remember the 'big five C's'? Well, now we look at words beginning with 'A'. In particular, attitude, appearance, and approach, and angry and awkward customers.

Generally, the correct attitude and approach, together with a smart appearance, will usually placate any angry or awkward customers. So often, though, staff involved in customer care show a lack of courtesy, are negative and unhelpful, are inattentive to a customer's needs, and far from enthusiastic about the product or service on offer.

It is important to retain a *positive* attitude when dealing with people, however difficult they are. With complaints, such a response will immediately signal that something will be done.

A poor attitude – rudeness and a lack of help – is one of three main reasons for customers complaining in the first place. The other two are:

- a bad product or poor service
- being kept waiting for service (or delivery) without any explanation.

There are others, like being given the wrong information, there being a misunderstanding about a customer's requirements, and some inconsistency in service (it was not up to the usual standard).

To return to our 'A' words. In addition to the positive attitude, the *approach* of the member of staff or manager to the complainant is also very important. It is vital to be confident, sure of your ground, including, of course, legal and regulatory requirements, when handling complaints. A wrong word or ill thought out promise can become extremely expensive to a company! The right approach also means having an excellent knowledge of the products and the operation of the business in order to discuss the complaint in a calm, rational manner.

Finally, it is important to properly *acknowledge* the complainant. Many are content to send more junior staff to meet the customer or to write a rather formal standard letter rather than handle the problem personally. Many complainants have become valued and regular customers simply because they were handled correctly when the complaint was first made – without worrying about time or more pressing administration duties!

The third 'A', *appearance*, is important in all care matters, not just complaints. Poor appearance of course is often the cause of complaints and certainly shows the customer exactly what standards to expect from an establishment. We have already talked of the all-important smile and eye contact, but appearance also embraces the 'turn out' – uniform or smart clothing *and* how it is worn.

The way in which the customer is addressed is also part of appearance. A dull monotone shows boredom and a lack of care, while being too bright and breezy can mean a lot of acting and insincerity. It requires practise and, yes, some element of a performance to get the voice just right, particularly when dealing with complaints; 'I am *so* sorry' can sound totally false if the tone is over the top!

Body language, too, has to be watched. We can be *saying* 'Sorry' with our mouths when our stance and bearing is saying 'We don't believe or trust you'. We can be saying 'Everything was all right when it left here', but the shifty glances and fidgeting hands tell the complainant that you *knew* that things were *not* right then!

Handling complaints is as skilled an art as caring itself. Indeed, it is closely linked to customer care. It is important to remember, too, that it is a unique occasion to the customer who is angry and upset enough to ring, write or call in person to complain. *They* do not know that they are the nineteenth complainant that morning – it matters to them. Many find it very hard to complain, so it is very important to handle things correctly.

There are a number of ways in which face-to-face or telephoned confrontation with an angry customer can be dissipated:

● *never argue* remain calm, listen, establish the facts

● *never be rude* this will only make things worse – if the complaint is face-to-face with you, remove them to a quiet corner where calm and peace can intervene

● *use silence* let the customer talk, which reduces the anger and has a calming effect – this should not be an 'angry' silence on your part, just show them that you are listening, not interrupting

● *use skilful question techniques to get at the facts* – try to strip out the essential facts from the anger and bluster.

There follow some simple do's and don'ts for handling complaints, but such difficult or time-wasting activities can be avoided by *anticipating* complaints *before* they happen. That is, if you have a problem, admit it, let the customer know what's happened and what you are doing about it – *communicate* – and, apart from some awkward ones, there should be no further problems. We all appreciate it if a company recalls a product because of a fault. We may not like it, but it shows caring. Similarly, we like to be told not just that the train is delayed for 10 minutes but *why* – we then have our curiosity satisfied and an excuse if we are late!

So, *do*:

● show interest – listen, treat with respect

● show empathy – how would you feel if this had happened to you?

● restate the problem back to the complainant – it confirms in your mind what you have been told, and reinforces the communication channel with the customer

● admit the problem – if there is one, and if a mistake has been made, an apology is needed – there is no point trying to wriggle out of an obvious shortcoming in your product or service

● ask the customer what they would want done – often this can be less than you have geared yourself up to provide, such as another cup of coffee, a replacement, a refund or credit note.

And *don't*:

- be defensive or aggressive – it may not be your fault

- say 'No' – there must be an added explanation to give the customer rather than just a straight denial

- assign blame – *you* will know who or what is responsible, but the customer doesn't need to; they just need to know that a mistake has occurred and you will put it right

- give the customer orders – be nice and friendly

- make unrealistic promises – this could make things worse and cause further complaints later

- leave the complainant in the lurch – keep them informed of progress in settling the complaint.

It is very important to show a lot of sincerity when handling complaints, including sympathy, purpose, and goodwill. It is always essential to reach an agreed and binding solution.

AVOIDING COMPLAINTS ARISING

Most complaints can and should be avoided by effective supervision and quality control – supervision that assesses the number of staff available to meet the need at busy times, that checks the way customers are greeted on the telephone or in person, that consults colleagues and subordinates about problems and proposals encouraging them to offer their own ideas and views (CICC again).

Complaints can be avoided, too, by having an effective after-sales service. We have all met the restaurant manager who dares you to complain and answer unexpectedly to the 'Everything all right?' question! So often – this sort of follow-up is handled in a very sloppy way. Customers don't *like* to complain, it is embarrassing and inconvenient – but they could be encouraged to comment if some openness and enthusiasm where shown to them to do so. After-sales activities take a lot of time, but they are very valuable. The analysis of questionnaires, write-ups of conversations from properly constructed questions, and so on will all produce a wealth of information with which to improve the product or service and avoid further complaint.

So, use your customers while you've got them – yes, actually encourage them to comment or complain and use the information gleaned to good effect.

HANDLING COMPLAINT LETTERS

As has been mentioned, many complaints or comments are received by telephone or letter – perhaps because many people don't want to be seen in person at a desk actually complaining!

In principle, the same rules, the same do's and don'ts apply, although, of course, written complaints take a lot longer to solve and, usually, can be a lot more serious. It is also important to remember that the written word can do far more damage legally if care is not taken to check the facts.

Looking at the written word in general, there is one main rule to stress: 'Let the care come through'. All too often, someone who is very open, frank, and friendly to a person's face can become long-winded, verbose, and boring in print! Many revert to jargon and hide behind a smokescreen of long words that are calculated to put off rather than encourage a customer to spend money.

Hotel brochures are often like this – packed full of facts about the age of the building, the length of the local golf course, which day is early closing and anecdotes about the annual Fayre, but forgetting to mention the bedroom facilities, leisure suite or size of the restaurant! Realizing this, a recent hotel owner on a customer care course set himself the task of rewriting his brochures from his guest's point of view!

This story is amusing but it contains a clue as to put care into the written word how to think like a customer. How would we feel if we were to receive such a letter or information about a company? Does it make sense, does it give the essential information in customer-friendly language? This not only applies to letters or brochures – memos, notices, instructions, all can be very formal and uncaring. So, 'think care' when writing!

HANDLING COMPLAINTS OVER THE TELEPHONE

The telephone is an important tool in our care armoury, and one that can cause more problems than any other because, so often, it is the first (and last) point of contact between the company and the customer.

It is essential to develop both a technique and a code of practice for using the telephone that allows the caring face of the company to be seen, even though (until video phones are widely available), this face is a disembodied voice coming through the receiver.

Figure 7.1 The ideal way to create the right impression while using the telephone

Again, the *technique* requires that the care elements come through any telephone conversation. When a customer is physically in front of us, do we gabble too quickly at them, do we lounge behind a desk, do we do other things while talking to them, do we shout at them, do we keep them waiting without any explanation? No, we *care* for them! The same should happen when using the telephone. Remember the following:

- poor posture affects speech, so sit upright when using the telephone
- eating, drinking or sucking pencils distorts our speech, as does putting the receiver under your chin while writing down a message
- speaking rapidly or loudly can easily distort the message or be annoying

To come across well then, over the telephone the technique is to *smile* – friendliness and warmth are communicated – to use clear language (there are no supporting visual aids), to listen with total attention, and always to remember that we are representing an organization that is efficient, willing, and caring (See Figure 7.1).

For a code of practice regarding using the telephone, here are some suggestions – all of which are common sense, but, unfortunately, much of it is forgotten regularly, like so many communications! For incoming calls:

1 answer as quickly as possible (a care standard), give the time of day, the number or name and see how you can help, but be careful – how many times do we get 'Good morning, Bloggs & Co., Sam speaking, how can I help?' all jumbled together and spoken very fast!?

2 listen carefully to the message and repeat back or question if you miss anything

3 obtain and use the caller's name

4 pass on the caller to the relevant extension or take a message if the person they need to speak to is unavailable

5 thank the caller and ring off quickly

6 ensure that the message is passed on – just making a note on a telephone pad is not sufficient, you need to check that it has been received *and* actioned.

For outgoing calls:

1 always prepare first: have the number, name, and message all available, with pad and pencil to note down responses

2 know who you are calling – their name and department or title, if possible.

3 speak as if you were there in person – remember to smile and to care for the customer.

4 obtain an answer or some promise of action, write down what was said immediately to avoid communication problems later

5 say 'Goodbye' and 'Thank you'

6 pass on any message, again ensuring that some action is taken.

Despite the many marketing activities of the telephone companies, using the phone is an expensive and often time-consuming activity, even though it is indispensable to modern company communications!

IN SUMMARY

• Good customer care can prevent many complaints.

• If handled correctly, and 'care-fully', many complainants can become regular and valued customers.

• Attitude, appearance, and approach are three vital ingredients of care, particularly when solving complaints.

• The telephone or the written word are often used for making or solving complaints. Both must be made user-friendly, with the care shining through.

• Like so many care activities, look at complaints, letters, brochures, and telephone procedures through the eyes of the customers. How would you feel?

Training and operational activities

· ·

STAFF

☞ **Looking at complaints**

Ask the group you have gathered together to think of any instances when they, as customers of other companies, have had to complain. What was wrong, why did they complain, what happened, were they satisfied with the action taken?

Build up a picture or list of common factors regarding the following kinds of questions.

● How was the telephone answered?

● How did the Manager/staff handle the complaint?

● How seriously was it taken?

● How long did it take to settle the problem?

● How were they treated?

● What do they feel about the company they complained about now? (Probe how long ago it happened.)

● What might have happened if they had been treated in a different way?

Also consider how written replies have been handled. There follow two letters that leave a lot to be desired regarding how a complaint should be answered. What is needed is a much more friendly and honest reply. This the trainees can attempt, using the content of the letters as a starting point.

Letter 1

Dear Sir/Madam

Poor service

Thank you for your letter of 15 June last and subsequent telephone conversation with my representative. We have now spent some time looking into the alleged incident of poor service at our Customer Service desk and have been unable to substantiate many of the faults you mention.

If you could provide us with further information – time of day, description of member of staff concerned, and so on – then we will be in a better position to investigate your problems.

We look forward to hearing from you.

Letter 2

Dear Mrs Jones

Further to your telephone call of last Thursday, I have now investigated the complaint you made against a member of the counter staff in our .... branch. The member of staff, Mr Fothergill, does not remember the incident, although he was very busy all afternoon. He certainly denies making any racist remarks and has always prided himself on the way he looks after all our customers; this is always stressed in our training sessions.

We will be looking again at the methods we use to deal with large numbers of customers at the counter and I hope that when you call again, you will not have any further grounds for complaint.

Points to bear in mind

1 In both cases, the customer's word has been doubted.
2 In Letter 1, the complainant has not been named and has been asked to substantiate the claim.
3 In Letter 2, is it right to name the member of staff concerned at this stage?
4 Although some admission of poor service has been made, in that some changes are to be made, no refund or voucher has been sent in goodwill. Would *you* go back?

The written word has to be very carefully considered when used in dealing with complaints. Once the trainees have rewritten the two letters above, use others from their own companies, blanking out any names, addresses or other distinguishing features. Have them appraise the replies.

Case study

REPLYING TO A COMPLAINT

Here are two letters from past guests of a hotel.

Read and study the letters. Then, decide how you will proceed to investigate the complaints and what has to be done. Draft suitable replies to the guests. Then decide what else might have to be done to improve care.

Now, probe how many have had to handle complaints while working in this company. Build up a picture, using questions such as the following.

● What was the complaint?
● Who handled it?
● How long did it take?
● What happened?
● What could have been done differently?
● Is the complainant still a customer?
● What lessons have been learned? (Such as that there is a lack of time or commitment, communication breakdown, bad mood of staff, or whatever.)

Letter 1

27 Carlton Road
Barset

The General Manager
.... Hotel

Dear sir

My husband and I recently stayed at your well-known establishment in order to attend the Annual Dinner and Dance of the Barset Yeomanry.

I had been looking forward to it a great deal, but, in the end, have been very disappointed at the poor service and lack of cleanliness of your overpriced bedrooms.

I have nothing against the reception area – they were very hospitable – nor the banqueting staff or restaurant – your breakfasts are still second to none. It was, I am afraid, the bedrooms that let you down. In detail:

a)   the bath and basin were dirty, with hair in the plug hole
b)   the dressing table and bedside tables were all dusty
c)   two mirrors were chipped
d)   the carpet was stained near the main bedroom door
e)   the hot water took several minutes to reach the tap
f)   the room was cold.

I could go on about the corroded shower, torn bedspread and dangerous kettle flex. The whole room gave the impression of decay and certainly a lack of care, maintenance, and inspection.

Due to my husband oversleeping (the wake-up call was late), I had no time to register my complaints on departure, although I told the Cashier of our disappointment. I hope you have now received her report.

I require an immediate explanation and apology. In no way does your hotel continue to offer value for money. May I suggest more money is spent on cleaning and guest care and less on distributing vast quantities of free giveaways in the bedrooms.

I await your reply.

Yours faithfully,

Susan Farnscombe

Letter 2

57 Sycamore Road
Hunstanton
Norfolk

The General Manager
.... Hotel

Dear Madam

Last weekend I attended the Annual Dinner of the World Wildlife Fund at your hotel, staying with friends, not at the hotel.

Within a few hours of leaving the Dinner, I experienced an attack of severe sickness, which lasted for some time and that necessitated my friends calling a doctor on a Sunday, and, ultimately, delaying my departure to Norfolk until Tuesday, which meant that I missed an important business meeting.

I have now returned home, still feeling a little weak, but now write to ask you:

1 whether or not you have received any other letter of this nature from other guests

2 in view of the doctor's opinion that it could only have been the food I eat at the Dinner that caused my illness, what do you propose doing about it?

One hardly expects such a problem from an hotel with your reputation, but, while I realize that certain things cannot be foreseen, I would have expected better control of food preparation.

My son is an Environmental Health Inspector and he, too, is very anxious to receive your urgent reply.

Yours faithfully,

Cyril Thickness

Your task

From all the activities so far, draw out some lessons and draw up a code of practice for the company or department. Consider communications – who handles complaints, what to do if someone complains – and how to deal with unnecessarily awkward customers! Below are 12 'rules of engagement' to help in this:

---

1 *be positive* – go into it to get a result
2 see the complaint as if you were the customer
3 *don't* take it personally, but *do* take it seriously
4 *listen* if face-to-face; *read and absorb* if written; *concentrate* if on the telephone
5 make it easy to complain – find a quiet corner
6 hear them out – be sympathetic, remember to provide *silence*, no arguing, no rudeness
7 don't justify or contradict, don't commit – it could be expensive
8 ask questions – get all the facts.
9 let them know what will happen and reassure them that something will be done
10 agree a course of action
11 see it through and see to the follow-up personally, check with the complainant
12 get a *result*, which is a happy customer!

From all the information gathered, agree with the staff how any complaints can be handled in a more *positive* way in the future. Draw up a code of practice that everyone can subscribe to and be involved with. To help with this, here is an example of the kinds of points to include.

● *Personal or by telephone*

- Get the person to calm down, if they are agitated, and explain the problem carefully.
- Have you got their name?
- Have you taken them aside so that matters can be discussed quietly?
- *Listen* and encourage the complainant to talk.
- Are you sure you have all the facts?
- Can you deal with this one or is it better passed up to a more senior person?
- Ask plenty of questions and *listen* to the replies.

- Keep calm. Don't argue or shout back.
- Tell them what you can or will do.
- Make sure you have their agreement.

● *Apologize*

- Confirm details of name, address, and so on, for a written follow-up.
- If authorized to, provide refund, credit or whatever.
- Remember, how would you feel?
- Follow up and/or see it through.
- Has complainant been written to/spoken to?
- Learn from each complaint.
- Always remember *care matters*.

● *For letters*

- Acknowledge within two days in a 'holding' reply.
- Fully investigate with relevant staff and management.
- If it is taking time, telephone the customer to explain why.
- Write a full explanatory reply, taking care to remember any legal pitfalls.
- Offer some recompense as necessary.
- If the customer is a regular, attempt to meet them at their next visit.
- Ensure similar problems don't recur by retraining or taking disciplinary actions.

Isolate typical examples of complaints and agree some action the staff can take to reduce these instances. It may be regarding delivery times, recurring problems with one product, information being received late, poor departmental communications that mean customers are not informed about what is happening or it may involve human problems like attitude, appearance, approach or simply a lack of ability to deal with customers. To supplement the discussion, carry out some structured role plays about typical complaints recently received.

Attitude, appearance, approach

Using these three 'A's, spend some time observing how staff are operating your customer care system. Use some form of check-list to award points and note shortcomings. Include the following kinds of questions for attitude.

● How courteously do they talk to/deal with people?

● How helpful are they?

● Do they show enthusiasm for the job or the customer?

● How well do they attend to customer needs, speed, efficiency, effort?

● Do they show a positive attitude?

● Consider also timekeeping, absence, willingness in the work, and so on.

For appearance, the following kinds of questions are useful.

● How smartly are they dressed, how neat is their uniform, and so on.

● Is their voice showing interest and enthusiasm?

● Do they smile or grimace?

● Do they establish eye contact?

● What about the non-verbal cues – does the body language say something different to what their mouths are saying?

For approach, use the following sorts of questions.

● How confident are they in dealing with customers?

● Do they quickly acknowledge the customer and use a name (once known)?

● What about the welcome/farewell, is it genuine?

● Test their knowledge of the company, the job, and the customers.

● How good are their communication skills?

These are just a few examples of questions that can be used to direct the observation. It will be a great help to use a video camera in this activity, suitably sited to avoid distraction or embarrassment. Tell the staff what you are doing and why. There may be some early reluctance and some extra activity at first, but, at busy times, the camera will be forgotten.

The resulting film will be a very valuable training tool, showing real-life examples, and is one of the quickest and easiest ways to show staff any good or bad practices.

Based on the results of your observations, you will have identified a number of training activities that it will be necessary to undertake quickly in order to capitalize on the research. It is likely, for example, that some will be slow to acknowledge or respond. They may not walk about in a positive way, not handle goods or products in a safe, careful or hygienic way, look down at the counter rather than at the customer, and be caught out giving incorrect information on a product or service.

Using the evidence of your check-list or video observations, put things right straight away, and have the staff compile their own personal action plans for attitude, appearance, and approach, ensuring that they report any results to you after an agreed time. It may help to use the following kind of table.

Action	How	By when	Checked	Help needed

Role plays

To supplement this work, have the group enact some role plays based on their own experiences. Alternatively you could try some of the following.

These role plays use short, sharp scenarios and give one side only. Mostly regarding complaints, they should be used to test the trainees' ability to cope with difficulties. At the same time, however, the trainer can assess their attitude and approach to the problems.

☞ Role play 1

Two people come to a bar to order drinks. One you immediately recognize as having been banned for drunkenness and causing trouble a week ago.

☞ Role play 2

A man comes to your reception desk to say he has seen two youngsters trying to break into a car in the staff car park.

☞ Role play 3

A telephone call is received (anonymously) to say that drugs are being traded in the public lavatories of the department store in which you work.

☞ Role play 4

A husband complains to you that his wife has just snagged her tights on a shop fitting.

☞ Role play 5

A rather bizarre-looking customer complains that your colleague (now taking a tea break) has been rude to her and won't serve her.

☞ Role play 6

Two regular drinkers complain to you that there is too much smoke in the bar and want something done about it.

☞ Role play 7

A customer ordering drinks from you claims that this round has cost £1.20 more than the last identical one.

☞ Role play 8

A regular jobbing builder comes into the builders merchants where you work to complain that less sand has been delivered than he ordered, but he has had to use it to get the job done.

☞ Role play 9

As a taxi company's telephone receptionist, you receive a call to say that the car ordered 20 minutes ago has not arrived. You know you sent the message to the driver but have had no acknowledgement since.

☞ Role play 10

At the bank where you work, a business customer comes in to say that his change (received yesterday) was £3.40 short over a number of different coinage denominations. Everything balanced last night.

Ability

If you find some staff are lacking in ability or knowledge at this stage, it will be necessary to undertake some retraining to bring these skills up to standard. What has to be done will, of course, depend upon the number of shortcomings identified.

Telephone skills

There are a number of external telephone skills training courses available, but it is just as effective to run short sessions in-house to check what skill levels staff have and correct any difficulties. Answering the telephone means a number of things to a company – all of them good course objectives. These are:

● creating the right impression from the first moment
● ensuring clear, concise, and informative communications

● selling the products and services, and knowing what they are and to whom they go for advice

● practical role plays, followed by drawing up individual action plans.

A typical half-day programme could therefore include:

● *first/last impressions* care in the voice or manner, creating interest and enthusiasm, finding out quickly what is wanted

● *communication* clear, concise, efficiency in, putting across the right company image

● *product knowledge* what the company's products are and their features and benefits

● *selling up* converting a call into more than just an enquiry, creating confidence in the company.

Role plays and action plans

For the practical element of the training it is possible to use a number of internal extensions without involving the main switchboard. There are also a number of 'training kits' available that include telephone receivers, tape recorders, and listening-in facilities.

Many role play examples from everyday life will come to mind, but as an extra resource, some are given in the Appendix at the back of this book.

There are many occasions when difficult situations have to be handled on the telephone, so, as an additional activity at this stage have the trainees 'brainstorm' some do's and don'ts for handling such occasions. (Remember, too, that customers often complain more when doing so on the telephone because they cannot be seen and so they find it less embarrassing to be forceful.)

Once completed, make the agreed list into an *aide-mémoire*. Some possible points to include in such a list of effective telephone skills for handling difficult situations are:

● *do's*

- apologize
- promise help
- get the facts (get help)
- keep the customer informed
  (pass on the facts)
- offer solutions
- ask the customer to choose
- act promptly
- apologize again
- notify the Manager
  (if it is a complaint).

● *don'ts*

- panic
- argue
- make excuses
- take it personally
- pass the buck
- grovel
- embarrass the customer
- delay
- promise what you cannot do
- hang up.

After-sales training points

Look at how staff follow up service – is it casual or concentrated, well meant or derisory? Watch what happens (perhaps making a video as before). How many customers actually reply or show interest, and are encouraged to comment or complain?

From the study, draw up a list of essential points to be worked on – from questioning technique to how to smile – and have staff concerned draw up an action plan for improving the service they give, with agreed dates for further assessment.

Look also at the after-sales literature and procedures. Does it not do anything for you, how many read it or use it? What could be done to help retain customers.

Again, role plays can be a useful training tool here – combining complaints with after-sales service to bring back an angry customer. For a more sophisticated approach though, and a longer training session for management, write a case study (based on recent real experiences) and ask for a considered solution to the problems posed by them.

Case study

Here is an example you can use.

THE DEMON COOKER

An account customer of the .... department store group, who has been loyal to the company for many years, comes into the shop to order a new kitchen. She takes advantage of the special offers available on a planning service and one of the company's planners visits her to agree on a plan and the equipment to go into the kitchen. Included is the current model of a free-standing electric cooker. Although there were superior models available, the customer was loyal to the maker of her previous, much older, cooker.

The order totalled £2500 and a deposit was paid. Six weeks later, the kitchen units arrive, but, because of a considerable workload, an additional fitter is employed (one who is not known well by the store, but who is related to one of the departmental managers).

By Saturday, 5 May, the cooker has not been delivered to the store, but it is promised for the Wednesday. The customer is delighted nevertheless that work can start on the rest of the kitchen on Monday, 7 May, and, indeed work commences then. The planner has promised the customer that a week is more than long enough to complete all the work.

On Tuesday, 8 May, the customer rings to complain that the fitter has just dropped one of the unit doors and badly gashed it – what can be done?

On Wednesday and Thursday she rings again to say that the fitter has not appeared and no message has been received. Also, she asks, where is the cooker?

After some difficulty, the fitter is contacted (there has been a family crisis) and he promises to be back on the job on the Friday, but it will be the end of the following week before he can complete it – the job is bigger than he thought.

The customer will accept a temporary replacement cooker until the new one arrives.

The planner now has a long weekend due, takes it and gets food poisoning! Returning to work on 21 May, and still feeling weak, the first call received is from this lady. She says that her kitchen is still not finished, the fitter has not turned up again, and she asks how much longer can this farce go on?

To add to the problems, in the post that day is a letter from the company that manufactures the cooker this lady ordered, saying that the company is in the hands of a receiver, and so no orders can be despatched for some considerable time. Another letter, opened during the planner's absence, informs the store that the oven ordered by the customer has been withdrawn because of safety problems with the main oven door!

Your task

Analyse the problem, then suggest a plan of action for placating the customer. Also, find out where the customer, store, and absent fitter stand in relation to the promised after-sales service that the company has legally agreed to provide? And what about the cooker? Plan the telephone conversations, letters and/or personal contacts you need to have with the cooker company, customer, and fitter. Think how your company would have handled this situation?

Operations

Many of the points covered in this chapter and results of these training exercises will highlight a number of operational changes that, if actioned, will improve the quality of care given to customers of the company.

For example, an analysis of the complaints received may highlight a number of regularly occurring faults in a product or service. It may, for example, point to a particular hotel bedroom or car park entrance, a specific delivery round or the design of part of a product. Such faults can only be solved by changing or adjusting the product or service to eradicate the cause of the complaints.

It is very important, too, to examine the literature provided for customers. Look at your brochures, standard letters, internal communications, memos – are they customer-friendly? Remember also notices, information sheets, instruction manuals – anything that is read by staff or customers which purports to 'sell' your care image. If it does not meet the criteria of being reader-friendly, uses excessive jargon or doesn't sell your image of care well enough, it needs to be changed at the earliest opportunity. The cost involved is repaid several fold in increased custom – the reward for telling the customer what they really want to know.

8

....

THE MANAGER'S ROLE

INTRODUCTION

We have now moved from the initial overview of customer care, through all the various processes, skills and competencies, to emerge, finally, at the manager's door. Managers have a crucial role to play in the customer care system. This chapter examines this role – looking at it primarily in the light of modern management thinking – and concludes with an exercise to help managers to evaluate their company's care policy.

LOOKING AT THE WHOLE PICTURE

The first crucial point is for a manager to recognize where customer care fits into the company's overall business policy. In the past, many companies tended to ride roughshod over their customers' needs and feelings, and ignored the training and development required by staff to enable them to service their customers effectively. This notion of 'the bottom line' being more important than pleasing the customer still appears today at times. Yet, customers are far more 'streetwise' than before, *requiring* the extra care that, for them, means a 'value for money' service.

So, it is vital to calculate how much extra profit and turnover can be gleaned from providing meaningful and effective care. This means being out and about on the shop floor or public areas – a 'see and be seen' policy. This is not to find fault and carry out endless checks on what is going on, but to *support* and *encourage* the front-line staff to give the best possible service.

It also means meeting and talking to the customers, finding out more about them, what they want from the company, what they think of the products, how they can be encouraged to tell others of your service (see Figure 8.1).

Some years ago, rumours abounded in the hotel industry about a General Manager who was seldom seen in public. He apparently passed his written decisions to his assistants under his permanently closed door! In contrast, one of the most successful General Managers, now running a prestigious London

Figure 8.1 Management needs to talk to customers too

hotel, is hardly ever in the office. Every guest knows him, every member of staff can talk to him, and his assistants don't want to leave or move up the career ladder. This hotel's results speak for themselves – guests returning time and again and personally advertising the establishment to colleagues and friends. Yet, in the vast majority of hotels, guests staying there or attending conferences often do not see members of senior management at all. Everything is left in the hands of staff who have not received sufficiently detailed training to enable them to make the right decisions.

The 'open door' policy banishes autocrats who constantly create fear and uncertainty among staff (and probably customers, too!) *Democratic managers* are the most successful in producing the best customer care as they both lead and are members of teams dedicated to serving the needs of those attracted to the warm, welcoming atmosphere such teams create.

This approach is being further nurtured by such initiatives as Total Quality Management, BS5750, Investors in People, and the accrediting of NVQs. In the latter case, what better way to achieve effective customer care than to first train staff to the requirements of the Level 3 Customer Service NVQ and have their efforts assessed by their own supervisors, who themselves have been trained as assessors!

To look at the process of the Investors in People Award for a moment, here first *commitment* from the top to the business aims and objectives of the company is communicated throughout the organization. Next, there is the *diagnosis* stage – what is actually happening, what sort of training and development is or should be occurring to meet these aims. This is followed by the making of an *action plan*, which maps out what has to be done to ensure that human resource development is linked to and can deliver the business objectives. Finally, how the whole process to be *evaluated* is agreed. Any business ignoring the care it gives its customers and its staff is unlikely to meet the standards expected and assessed to ultimately achieve this Award.

Similarly, quality systems, which set standards to be met, have to involve the staff at all levels and, therefore, also have to consider the care given to the customers.

The result of all these initiatives is that companies, more and more, are looking hard at their management structures. Already, whole levels are being stripped away, staff are being trained in empowerment, and there is considerable emphasis on the team approach. These flatter organizations are beginning to achieve staggering changes, not only in working practices, but also in the quality of service being given to customers, so much so that the service and the product is now *customer-driven*. The 'customers' shoes' have now begun to walk on to the factory floor!

The manager's role, therefore, is no longer one of being the rule *maker*, but of being the rule *enhancer*; not the autocrat forcing down tablets, but the democrat sharing in the pleasures and difficulties of pleasing the customer and shaping the policy in order to make it customer-sensitive.

This requires consultation with all concerned, particularly staff and customers, so that it can lead to clear care-driven decisions being made. Staff are happy because they are receiving the right training and so providing the correct service to customers because their needs and wants have been satisfied.

Such success cannot be guaranteed if the company providing the care is too results-driven. Too many corners will be cut, too many rules enforced, and, sadly, too many customers needs ignored – all in pursuit of the highest profit. Profit and results, though, can come more easily to a customer-driven company simply because the customer is getting what they want and so returns frequently to receive more of the same. Reputation and good service is worth far more than clever advertising of the product!

So, we are back again to the 'good staff care equals good customer care' equation, but now there is a third element – 'good management involvement'. This must occur at all levels of the organization, providing the focal points for staff and customers to come to if and when a problem arises (these should be very important if the system is working effectively!) Involvement also creates the incentive for staff to give of their best – they want to be noticed by their team leaders, (as managers are now frequently called), to be allowed to have their say in the running of the department or section, and to quickly feed back any problems they have identified. Such a communication exchange cannot occur if the manager is permanently at a desk, wrestling with computer printouts and head office policy decisions!

Figure 8.2 The quality of the teamwork leads to excellent customer care, which leads to an excellent financial situation

Mention of incentives brings us neatly on to their use and misuse in customer care. Again, so often incentives, like bonuses for filling the order book or hotel bedrooms, can lead to a *lessening* of customer care rather than an increase because of the pressure created to achieve results. The greatest incentive driving good staff caring for customers properly is that of being able to serve and please happy customers and be paid a generous salary for it because their good care has brought in good profits.

'Incentive' also means recognizing excellent service with a more permanent reward scheme rather than one-off payments. It means sound management back-up and support rather than a once-a-day inspection!

So, what about *evaluation*? The management role here is, again, the cycle of control outlined in Chapter 4. It means keeping a watching brief on all things that are happening and adjusting or reviewing procedures if things go wrong.

Evaluating care is not easy; so many people and events are involved, and so many customers do not wish to contribute to oral questions or formal questionnaires. Analysis of complaint letters (and, of course, compliments) can be of great value, as can logging repeat business and recommendations. In the end, it comes down to how much the business increases can be attributed to the provision of good customer care.

The communications exercise and personal activity overleaf will be of some assistance in this. It is vitally important that the results of any evaluation are passed on to the staff concerned, along with all the compliments received.

In summary therefore, we are back again to our CICC approach, which is to *consult* with the front-line staff, to be *involved* with them as they handle all their dealings with customers, and to be *involved* with the customers themselves. Staff should see their manager not just as a contact name, but a real person who is approachable, and knows their likes, dislikes, and requirements. This brings about *commitment* from everyone – loyalty, enthusiasm, and a willingness to please and be pleased with the product and service provided. Finally, *communications* is the real key to customer care. Being open and honest, telling or giving the full story to everyone in order to build up trust, pride, and – that vital word – *belief* in the job, the company, the service, the product, and the people (see Figure 8.2).

A communications exercise

This is to be completed by all managers and discussed by staff (and customers). Answer all the questions as honestly as possible.

1 What is your company's/department's policy on customer care?

2 Do you have an agreed definition of care? Is it known by everyone? How often do you test this?

3 Do all the staff and managers know who the customers are and what they *expect* from the service or care they give them?

4 Are all staff and managers clear about what their jobs involve with regard to customer care? Are such duties and responsibilities regularly reviewed, evaluated, and discussed?

5 Is there a departmental/company plan for improving or raising standards of customer care? How often is this plan reviewed?

6 How are care standards monitored and reviewed? Does this review include everyone involved in customer care?

7 If this results in new standards, how are they introduced? Does it include all staff in the care communication map?

8 How good are your communications? Does *everyone* have a chance to be involved? Does it flow top to bottom, bottom to top, and across all levels?

9 Do your communications about care include your customers? How do you tell them about your care standards? Do you have dialogue with regular customers to check the care provided?

10 If and when shortcomings occur, how is remedial training handled? How quickly is it organized? How is it tested and evaluated? Are records kept?

11 How often do you carry out care training with all staff in order to maintain standards? Is this a fully democratic process, that is, *all* levels receive training?

12 How do you evaluate your customer care policy? How often is this done? Who receives the results and who is involved in the process?

13 Having evaluated, what happens next? Who instigates changes/improvements and what checks are made?

14 Are you fully satisfied that the care you provide for your managers and staff is the best available?

15 Are you fully satisfied that the care you, your managers, and staff provide for your customers is the best available?

Add further questions to suit your own company needs and arrange to ask all these questions again and again to ensure that the care process in the company is constantly checked, reviewed, and evaluated by a fully involved and committed team.

A personal activity

● ●

This activity is to be carried out by every manager and, if considered useful, every member of a team dealing with customers.

How it works

First, sit down alone and answer each of the questions below as honestly and as fully as possible.

When you are satisfied with the answers, talk them over with a colleague and vice versa. Be as open and honest as possible on both sides.

Next, gather the team together and make a list of all the activities that the team members consider they do well – the strengths.

Then, make another list of all the activities that are not being achieved so well – the weaknesses.

From the two lists it is then possible to:

● see who is good at which activities and who can be given more opportunity to exercise these strengths when dealing with customers

● see what weaknesses have to be worked on in order to make the team even more efficient

● plan a development programme of training to ensure that care of the customer is really made a priority by everyone and becomes a major strength for the team or the company.

The questions

1 How constructive am I when dealing with my front-line team? Do I encourage them to perform well and think for themselves?
2 How productive am I? Do I make the best use of my time when talking to/dealing with customers or staff?
3 Am I an ideas person and look for good care solutions or just accept what I have to do or am told to do?

4 Am I an organizer – do I think of both staff and customers as people when organizing work or activities?

5 How good is my administration? Does it get in the way of good care?

6 How methodical am I? Do I plan ahead or just respond in a crisis, so that care suffers?

7 What sort of caring person am I?

8 How well do I communicate? Do my staff understand what I want from them in terms of care and service?

9 How well do I communicate up, down, and across? Do I properly reflect the best results and successes of my team when looking after customers?

10 Do I involve my team sufficiently in decision making so that they can reflect this knowledge when dealing with customers?

11 Do my staff trust me? Do I care for them?

12 Do all my team know what their care objectives and targets are?

13 Do I listen to others (staff and customers) and take note of their opinions, feelings?

14 Do I ensure that my own and my team's care and service priorities are one and the same?

15 Do I offer enough help, care, and support to my team and to my customers?

16 How well do I delegate? Is it enough, too much, do I allow my team to provide enough customer care?

17 Do I praise as well as blame when receiving feedback about customer service?

18 How available am I to offer help and encouragement?

19 Are the care and service goals I set my team reasonable and challenging?

20 How much commitment to care and service do I obtain from my team?

21 Do I get fully involved in the problems of my team? Is it enough?

22 How do I motivate others to provide the best care?

23 Do I share success and failure with everyone?

24 How good am I at caring and service with regard to both customers and staff?

25 Do I earn my place on my team?

Appendix
Case studies and role plays

HOW TO USE CASE STUDIES AND ROLE PLAYS

The ideal case study or role play is a real-life example written up to either be discussed or played out in front of observers. In this way what actually happened can be explained after the role play has finished or the case study has been reported on.

Always allow plenty of time for discussion of the case study and feedback – preferably using two or more groups to present their different solutions.

With role plays, draw out from the observers (and the actors) as much as possible about the cases enacted – reactions, body language used, the result, and so on. Try to reach a consensus about what actually should have happened.

CASE STUDIES

Case study 1

J. W. Frogwell and Sons is a well-established tour operator and coach company in the Midlands. Founded by Grandfather Frogwell in the 1930s, the company has grown from a small 'school run' coach travel provider to become, for many years, the leader in the neighbourhood for English and Continental tours.

To cope with this expansion, ten years ago, the company opened a number of small travel agency shops and, because of the friendly approach of the staff and the company's reputation, have held their own against bigger national competitors. The company is still family owned – the Managing Director is George Frogwell – and has a small Board controlling the operations. Much power is passed down to the managers of the shops, agencies, and coach company. They have a system of communication that takes note of all feedback from customers.

However, during the past few months, trade has started to drop, but there is no real apparent reason for this. The directors put it down to the recession, but then one overhears a conversation in a pub that mentions damaging rumours about a coach driver. The local radio station, without checking with the company, starts to broadcast a vicious piece about poor service and rudeness on a coach trip to the Dutch bulb festival, then several complaint letters start to arrive that seem to throw up all sorts of customer care problems.

The radio report also starts a concentrated public 'have a go' session in the travel shops and trade begins to slump badly.

You are a member of a hastily summoned management group charged with investigating the problems and given the power to act quickly.

Your tasks

Outline how you would go about this investigation. Also, suggest how you could restore confidence in the group by re-establishing good care techniques. Then, draw up an effective customer care programme to ensure that standards are maintained, with particular emphasis on the complaints procedures being quickly actioned.

Case study 2

(For study in syndicates, with a full plenary presentation and discussion.)

The Sloan Hotel Group is a long-established company, trading in the upper end of the market. Founded by Sir Forbes Sloan, some 95 years ago, the first (Sloan) Hotel was built to cater for the needs of the many clients of Sloan and Company Limited, a major beer and spirits company, first founded in 1623 by Sir Forbes Sloan's ancestor.

The Group now has seven establishments that, between them, claim to cater for a very wide clientele. The flagship is still the Sloan Hotel itself, and it remains at the upper end of the market. Four others were bought from another company ten years ago and they now produce the bulk of the Group's revenue as they cater for a very wide cross-section of clients, including businessmen, tourists, and commercial travellers.

Three years ago, the Group took over another drinks company, and, coming with it, was an apartment block with an up-market restaurant and a group of seaside chalets/guest apartments that were used by members of staff and let to the public when they were not being used by staff.

The hotels part of the business has always been something of a secondary interest to the Sloan family – no separate Board of Directors has ever been appointed and much of the decision making has been left to the individual managers of the hotels. As a result, there is a wide difference in quality standards, with no recognizable company image, particularly regarding the care of customers.

There has, in fact, been a very high turnover of staff, both at management level and at the lower end. However, many of the heads of departments have been with the company for 15 to 20 years, resisting any attempt to change attitudes or update services.

Six months ago, predators appeared on the scene, intent on buying the company. As part of its defence, the main Board brought in a new executive management team, giving them the specific brief of raising the image of the group.

The Chairman personally drew up the plans for this new Board and expects results quickly as he doesn't want to lose the hotels or the beer and spirits company.

Your task

You are that management group charged with:

- producing a statement of intent regarding quality throughout the Group
- drawing up a plan to instigate a quality customer care drive in each hotel
- putting forward suggestions regarding:
  - a guest profile survey
  - investigating guest reactions to the hotel of their choice
  - planning what action has to be taken as a result of these first two points
- producing plans for working parties and training programmes on customer care in each hotel.

You are to make a full presentation to the Chairman, with each member of the Group taking an active part.

Case study 3

Nought Degrees Limited is an expanding company providing fridges and freezers to the domestic market. It takes a small, franchised space in local grocery stores to display the cabinets and provides a percentage of the sales price to the shopkeeper when one is sold.

All goods are despatched by road from a central warehouse in the Midlands, using self-employed drivers. In addition, the company now has a number of service engineers who carry out installations, repairs (under guarantee), and some other electrical repairs – an extra service just started recently.

The company is owned by a family (Mr and Mrs Stocks and their two sons), but now employs nearly 50 people, mostly in distribution, franchise sales, and as service engineers.

From the early days, Mr Jim NcNaugton looked after the distribution of the cabinets and the organization of the engineers. An old family friend, he kept things on a very tight rein and ensured that the family's insistence on good care shone through every transaction.

Unfortunately, he was taken seriously ill six months ago, and, after a slow recovery, decided that retirement was the safest thing.

During the time he was ill, Mr Stocks has coped as well as possible, but, after a struggle to find a replacement, engages Mr O'Halloran to take on the post vacated by Mr McNaughton.

Mr O'Halloran is a very different person. He is not able to train staff and persuades Mr Stocks to engage Julie Wright to take on this job. Meanwhile, he has many of the self-employed drivers' backs up with his domineering attitude.

Soon complaints (so far unheard of) begin to find their way on to Mr Stocks' desk. Customers are complaining of late delivery and poor installation service, local shop-keepers want the cabinets removed because no one comes to see them, and many of the drivers want to drop the Nought Degrees contract from their schedules.

Then, more complaints are received by telephone concerning the rudeness of the staff at the distribution depot and of the delivery drivers. Mr Stocks has to act quickly to save his company.

Your task

As Mr Stocks, draw up a plan of action aimed at solving the problem. Consider the complaints, the current system of distribution, and so on, and why the previously good care of both staff and customers has suddenly become a bad apple.

Discuss in syndicate and make a report.

Guidelines

A case of poor staff care from the top affecting all arms of the business? What's happened to the training? Can customer care work so far from the centre?

Case study 4

You have just been appointed Customer Services Manager for a new fast food restaurant chain, Happy Baps Limited.

The company is opening seven new restaurants in the South West of England early in the summer in order to get the name known among holidaymakers from other parts of the country. The plan, then, is to have sufficient local trade to keep the restaurants going in the winter while selected sites in the Midlands and North are developed.

The owner Microbite Limited, want to provide quick but efficient service, and provide top-flight customer care, based on a traditional English rather than an American mode. Excellent service points, providing good eye contact between customers and staff, are being installed and the restaurant seating is designed to encourage people to enjoy their meal in relaxing surroundings.

The Chairman of Microbite Limited, George Russell, briefs you on his vision for the company – long-service staff, eager to work for the company and please the customer. Best care for staff and customer is essential.

He wants your plans for seeing out this vision within the week.

Your task

To draw up customer care and staff standards for the company. Also, to suggest training schedules for each restaurant and an outline contact for staff training, and draw up a code of practice and briefing document for the managers to use.

Any other suggestions you may have for ensuring success, including how the training will be managed (say, appointing a Training Officer or making it manager-led), evaluation of care, and how many checks may be made on the service given.

ROLE PLAYS

☞ Role play 1

Customer

You are a foreign tourist new to Britain with little English. So far you have come to Heathrow, then taken a bus to _____. Now you are looking for help and directions to a bank, a hotel, and other facilities. The Post Office counter in this shop has a friendly face behind it. Take things from there.

Staff

You are on duty at the Post Office counter in a small shop on a busy day. You are approached by a foreigner carrying luggage and looking confused. What do you do next?

☞ Role play 2

Customer

You have purchased a number of items from a shop, totalling £3.27. You pay with a £10 note as you want to keep two £5 notes for your grandchildren's treat. The assistant gives you change and you leave the shop. Outside, you realize that your change is short of a £5 note, so you go back inside to the same assistant, who you see after several other customers have been served. You explain, but she says it was a £5 note you tendered. Take it from there.

Staff

It is a busy day in a shop and you are rushed off your feet. Suddenly a customer you served a few minutes ago is back in front of you saying they are short of £5 in change. You are pretty convinced it was a £5 note (not a £10) that was tendered, but you are busy and a bit on 'auto pilot' because of some domestic worries. You try to explain.

☞ Role play 3

Staff

You have watched a person wandering around your shop. It seems possible that they are thinking of shoplifting. You are convinced, after a further period of time, that something has been slipped into a bag. You approach the customer.

Customer

You are waiting for your nephew to arrive, who is coming by bus. To waste time, as the bus is late, you spend time in the local shop, looking at the goods for sale. There are several books of interest. Suddenly you are aware of a member of staff very close to you with a rather menacing expression.

☞ Role play 4

Customer

You have arrived at the coast for a short break. Today has been a bad day – several things have gone wrong. When the cashier at the local attraction tells you the price of admission, you think the price is steep and 'explode'.

Staff

You are the cashier on duty at the local attraction. A harassed person with a party of children suddenly attacks you verbally about the price of admission. There is a queue and the complex is busy – you have to do all you can to sort things out.

☞ Role play 5

Customer

You have heard a lot about the ice-cream as well as the facilities at the local swimming pool, so take your children along for a treat. Having paid your entrance fee and sorted out the children, you go in search of the ice-cream kiosk, only to find that it is closed. You find a member of staff and complain strongly.

Staff

You are a fairly new part-timer at the local swimming pool. Having been on duty only a few minutes, you are accosted by an irate customer complaining that there are no ice-creams. (You remember a conversation you overheard earlier in the office about late delivery of ice-cream and know that the kiosk has run out.) Take it from there.

☞ Role play 6

Customer

You are 83 and seldom come into town. Today, you have struggled in to meet your daughter, but aren't sure now where she said to meet her. The surroundings are a little unfamiliar. You approach a local security guard for directions.

Staff

You are the security officer of the local shopping centre and the day has been a bad one – shoplifting, disturbances, staff shortages. Now an elderly person is approaching you looking a bit confused.

☞ Role play 7

Customer

You have rung a hotel to make a lunch booking. Time is precious and your annoyance increases the longer it takes them to answer the phone. You are about to ring off when the phone is answered, very pleasantly, but she is unsure what to do. She goes to find someone else so you are kept waiting again. Your temper starts to go when another voice answers.

Staff

The trainee in your department has answered the telephone and comes back to you saying the caller wants to make a complaint. You prepare yourself for a difficult conversation.

☞ Role play 8

Customer

Recently, arriving in town for the day, your young son had been rather ill in the car. Seeing a shop you rush in to try to buy him some cheap but necessary clothes to change into. The car is on a yellow line and your husband is a bit fed up. You can't find an assistant and the shop is strange to you. You start to panic and feel annoyed. Suddenly an assistant emerges from a door.

Staff

You are fairly new to the job, the morning has been a little fraught, but a nice cup of coffee and a chat about last night's party have revived you. In something of a daze, you come back on to the shop floor to be met by a person in something of a panic.

☞ Role play 9

Staff

You have to urgently price up some face flannels to replace quickly depleting stocks. The shop is busy and this is the third time today that you have had to do some pricing, which you hate. You didn't join to do all this menial work – you want to serve customers. You are in a bad mood, there is a long time until lunch, and, suddenly, you have some customer coughing at you. Something 'gives' inside you!

Customer

You have come into the shop to buy some towels similar to some you purchased three years ago. After wandering round looking at the stock, you can't find anything suitable, but would like to get some help. There is an assistant with her back to you and, despite standing by the counter for several minutes, nothing happens, so you cough.

☞ Role play 10

Customer

You have heard a lot about this store's service, stock, display – all of it good – so you decide to check things out for yourself. On arrival, your information seems to be accurate. Although there are one or two staff talking to each other, the store is busy, displays are attractive, and there is a good range of products. So, you decide to try out the system. Seeing a young assistant, you ask her about a rather difficult to obtain product (choose anything you consider would be a test!)

Staff

You have only been working in this store for three days and, despite some basic induction training, you are still unfamiliar with what goes on. Your supervisor asks you to get some more goods from the stockroom. On the way there, you are accosted by a rather officious customer.

Note The remaining role plays have an 'open' theme: the 'staff' are required to play their roles as if working for their own company.

☞ Role play 11

You have heard that restaurant 'X' is good, but you have always gone to a rival establishment to entertain your business guests. You now decide to give this one a try, to see how you are 'sold' the facilities.

☞ Role play 12

Your daughter is getting married next year and you now have to gather information about all the various services that will be necessary to select a florist, taxi company, caterer, photographer, printer, wedding list at a department store, bridal outfitter, and so on. You decide that the one selected for each of these functions will be the one offering the best care and have a friendly approach to your requests (you are not necessarily looking for the cheapest). You start telephoning.

☞ Role play 13

You and your partner have eaten well in a local branch of a restaurant chain. One dish seemed to have a strange taste, but the dish was new to you (and your partner). Everything else was fine. Then, in the night, you are both ill. In the morning, still feeling dreadful, you ring the restaurant to ask for an explanation. First, the telephone is engaged, then there is a delay in answering. You wonder whether to approach the chain's Head Office, but have one more try and get through.

☞ Role play 14

You are working at the counter in a bank. A young person comes into the branch, looking very distraught. You discover that they have lost their credit cards, but so far you don't know how or where.

☞ Role play 15

On duty at the Playhouse's box office, it is quiet because the play that's on at the moment is popular and so most of the seats have been sold. Then, someone rings up and, in a rather belligerent fashion, demands that you exchange four of the most expensive seats for six cheaper ones, so that they can bring their friends. No seats are available at that price. (This is useful telephone role play for a good 'actor' playing the belligerent customer.)

☞ Role play 16

You are the last person on duty at the local bus station and, just as you are locking up, following the departure of the last bus, a frightened-looking young girl arrives to catch it. She explains that she only has enough money for the bus, it's a six-mile journey, and she can't afford a taxi.

☞ Role play 17

You are working behind the public bar at a local and popular inn. It is extremely busy with several office parties. After serving a big party, a customer, who has already had a lot to drink, offers you what you think is a forged £10 note.

☞ Role play 18

You are working at the control desk of a town centre taxi company (near pubs, the railway station, and so on). A well-dressed man comes in, demanding a taxi immediately. Currently they are all out, taking customers to a wide variety of destinations; the first one is not expected back until 1.00 am (30 minutes after your shift ends at 12.30 am) and it is now 12.15 am. When you tell him this, he becomes abusive, saying he knows your Managing Director and he will make it his business to inform him of your inefficiency tomorrow. You do have your own car, but your night relief has not yet arrived.

☞ Role play 19

You are alone at the reception desk of a local Leisure Centre. Suddenly, the door bursts open and a young woman appears. She has lost her child and is beginning to panic. Apparently her son was last seen near the swimming pool. He is two years old.

READY MADE ACTIVITIES RESOURCE PACKS

Developing your Staff
Selling Skills
Customer Care Skills
Negotiation Skills
Presentation Skills

In a high pressure environment you need to bring your team up to speed quickly and effectively. Waiting for the right course can waste time.

The *Ready Made Activities Resource Packs* give you access to material to develop your own skills and those of your staff in vital areas such as finance, negotiation and customer care.

You can see how simple it is to improve the skills of your staff and save your company thousands of pounds by completing the training yourself. It couldn't be easier with our unique new *Ready Made Activities Resource Pack* – and you don't have to be an expert or even have any training experience to use them!.

These special versions of the Ready Made Activities series come with the full endorsement of the Institute of Management and are available in a Ringbound Presentation Folder containing all the information you could need to present the new skills to your team.

All the *Ready Made Activities Resource Packs* come complete with
- Overhead Transparencies – impress your colleagues and your bosses with a professional presentation
- Free Video – reinforce the message or open your sessions with this ice-breaker
- Photocopiable Handouts – give your staff the key points of your presentation to take away and refer to again and again.

All this and more for only £120.00*

Available direct from Pitman Publishing
Telephone 071 379 7383 or fax 071 240 5771

*Price correct at time of going to press but is subject to change without notice